People are talking about

Coincidences:
Touched by a Miracle

෴ ෴ ෴ ෴

"Prize winning author, Antoinette Bosco, has done it again! If you like well-written stories about well-known people, this book will engage and satisfy you. I found the central idea fascinating: a few moments in a person's life can change their direction and their destiny. Are they coincidences or miracles? The reader is free to choose. You'll love this book."

Fr. John Catoir
Author of the video program, *Prayer Made Simple and Joyful*
Immediate past director of the Christophers

"In her book, *Coincidences: Touched by a Miracle,* Antoinette Bosco continues to do what she has done exceedingly well in the past. With a blend of story, theology, and lived experience, she invites and encourages readers to reflect on the coincidences in their lives. She begins her book by quoting one of the great mystics who said, 'the sacred is in the ordinary.' She goes on to describe in a wide variety of engaging personal stories how singular events become transformative meeting points between people and God."

Fr. Allan Weinert, C.Ss.R.
Editor, *Liguorian Magazine*

"Antoinette Bosco explores an uncharted realm through stories that lift the spirit. It is no coincidence, this sense of grace that comes from allowing oneself to be drawn into these inexplicable yet common occurrences that so enrich our lives."

Stephan Rechtschaffen
Omega Institute for Holistic Studies
Author, *TimeShifting*

"When a well-established author like Toni Bosco takes the time to listen to the 'inner' story of the known and less known, she's bound to hear things that are worth sharing. Toni connects us to God in a believable way. She takes the prayers, struggles, hopes, and dreams of our lives and asks us to remember if we ever saw the hand of God guiding us. Toni Bosco inspires and challenges. Her book is a thoughtful gift for people of prayer."

Monsignor Tom Hartman, The 'God Squad'

"Luckily for Antoinette Bosco, more than coincidence sends people's stories of serendipity her way...[She's] a lightning rod for people who think the little twists in their lives are more than throws of the dice...She has assembled these stories in a seamless collection that makes a point: A coincidence may be more than you think."

Larry Witham, *The Washington Times*

"Coincidences, or miracles with a small "m," or God-incidences as this books calls them, have a way of making the reader feel inspired and uplifted, and very in tune to noticing the simple yet phenomenal things that are happening around us."

Pat Conway, *New Milford Spectrum*

"This is the type of book you will find yourself reaching for when you need confirmation about the coincidences in your own life. It is intriguing and inspiring."

Jean Sands, *The Register Citizen*

"Bosco weaves into her pages many tales about how coincidences have affected her own life. And constant in all of her stories is the power of God's love. Her book makes a strong case for 'remarkable coincidences,' and it tells some beautiful stories..."

Peggy Weber, *Catholic News Service*

"What is so uplifting about Toni Bosco's new book is that it pushes skepticism to one side. It shows that what is important about experiences of synchronicity is not whether or not they point to divinity that shapes our ends, but rather that coincidences so often change people in ways that make their lives better."

Alistair Highet, *The Litchfield County Times*

"This book offers both delight and amazement!"

Arlene Goetze, *Catholic Women 's Network*

"The stories in this short and lucid book offer compelling testimony. Even if you don't subscribe to Ms. Bosco's view that these events may have been orchestrated by God, her book is a wonderful read."

Jack Sheedy, *Tri-State Compass*

Coincidences
Touched
BY A
Miracle

Antoinette Bosco

TWENTY-THIRD PUBLICATIONS
Mystic, CT 06355

Dedication

It is with gratitude that I dedicate this book
to all the caring people from
so many different parts of the country
who have shared their stories of coincidence with me.

Second printing 1998

Twenty-Third Publications
185 Willow Street
P.O. Box 180
Mystic, CT 06355
(860) 536-2611
(800) 321-0411

ISBN 0-89622-749-9
Library of Congress Catalog Card Number 97-61921
Printed in the U.S.A.

Acknowledgments

Writing a book begins with a desire, but sometimes it takes a catalyst to get you to actually begin putting the words together. For being this catalyst, I credit Neil Kluepfel, publisher of Twenty-Third Publications, who had the graciousness and trust in me to call and ask if I had another book that I thought he would be interested in. I did. It was this one, and he responded with a heart-warming yes. This is my third book for Neil, and I can say from firsthand experience that when it comes to publishers, he is the best!

And working with editor Gwen Costello and publicist Bill Holub is another decided pleasure for any writer fortunate enough to be linked with Twenty-Third Publications.

My gratitude goes to all the wonderful people who have sent me their coincidence stories over the years. Most of these have been in reponse to requests I made through my syndicated column carried weekly by Catholic News Service. But these people did not merely write me a story. Each one also shared a bit of their hearts with me, and for this I shall ever be deeply touched.

I must also thank my family—brothers and sisters and children—for the encouragement and support they have given me every step of the way, and for their stories, too.

As the line says, "My cup runneth over," from the riches all these people have given me.

Contents

Coincidences

Touched by a Miracle

Introduction

No matter who we're talking to these days, something is likely to come up in conversation that begins, "By coincidence…" Then as the story is told, you both agree that this happening had to be more than just coincidence. Before long you're probably sharing the same questions: Can we really attribute coincidences only to chance, particularly when these may have a profound effect on a person? Or can it be that a more powerful force is at work here?

I have been fascinated by tales of coincidence ever since I was a child. This was because of a true story my mother told me when I was no more than seven years old. It had happened to her back in 1926. She told me it was a coincidence, and that word stuck in my head. The setting was the baptism of my older sister Rosemary when she was an infant. For people of Italian heritage, baptisms were events that were held with verve and celebration. As was the custom, most gave money gifts for the baby. One of my parents' friends gave cash, but in a more festive package—a five-dollar gold piece. That was a lot of money back then, especially for a struggling young couple without much to call their own.

My mother somehow felt a strong urge to send that gold piece to her mother, who lived one hundred miles away. My father agreed, and she mailed it off to her mother immediately. The day it arrived, my grandmother was in shock. It seems she too had been given a five-dollar gold piece in payment for some work, and that very day, she had sent her coin to her own mother in southern Italy. Coincidence?

I never forgot that story. To a seven-year-old, it sounded more like magic or a fairy tale. But as years went on, I became amazed at how often I would hear of surprising occurrences in someone's life that were blithely shrugged off as chance happenings, even when they may have triggered an actual change in the direction of that person's life. Then there would be the incidents that were merely humorous or unusual that would be written off as just another coincidence.

One of these incidents happened to my daughter Mary in December 1990. She lives in New York City and that month had been in a bookstore to buy some books as a Christmas present for my son Peter. Since this was the Christmas shopping season, the store was full of people and Mary had a long wait as the line to the cashier moved slowly forward. She had finally gotten to second place when a tedious delay began. The woman just ahead of her was complaining that she couldn't find a book she just had to have, and she wasn't going to move on until she got some help. Because Mary was right behind her, she could not help overhearing what was going on.

The woman was holding a newspaper clipping with a review of a book called *Be Friends of God, Spiritual Reading from Gregory the Great*. She was frustrated, she said, because she had been unable to locate the book, written by Brother John Leinenweber and published by Cowley Publications in Cambridge, Massachusetts. The clerk was apologetic, but insisted he was unable to help her.

Mary peered over the woman's shoulder, glanced at the clip, and, to her surprise, saw that the book review was one I had written for *The Litchfield County Times*. She greeted the woman and told her that, though it might seem an impossible coincidence, the author of the book review was her mother. She gave the woman my phone number so she could call me for help in locating the book. She did call, and I did help. The woman told me she had seen the book review and had wanted to get the book as a present for the priest who had married her and her husband in a church named for—you guessed it—St. Gregory the Great.

Mary and I then wondered, was this just a coincidence or was there another force at work? There are millions of people in New York City. Was it meant to be that this woman and my daughter would be in the same place at the same time on the same day? And, if so, who makes these strange arrangements that we come up against so often in life and that we can call by no other name than "coincidence"?

After this occurrence, I decided to write one of my syndicated columns on this phenomenon of coincidence. To my surprise and delight, Thomas J. Dermody, editor of *The Catholic Post* in Peoria, Illinois, not only carried my column, he did something special with the piece. He ran a box at the end of my column headed "Share Your Coincidences," explaining, "Like Antoinette Bosco, we are intrigued by such chance happenings. We would like to carry a feature story on the subject, and we need your help."

Mr. Dermody asked readers to share similar stories that they feel "may have the hand of God at work." He received many responses, and published them in the newspaper's May 13, 1991 edition. He sent me a copy and I had smiles and tears as I read these accounts which many readers, Mr. Dermody said, called "God-incidences." They all felt that in the face of a phenomenon not readily explainable, one has to ask if another, more powerful, Force—and they capitalized that word—is at work.

After this feature was published in *The Catholic Post,* I decided that one day I wanted to write a book about coincidences, raising the question, as Mr. Dermody did, of whether these are not rather "God-incidences." I started asking people about coincidences in their lives and also began noting how often coincidence is found in history. I soon found myself collecting stories, and now I am sharing these tales with all who read this book.

Some may believe that there is nothing at all to coincidences, that they are just ordinary things occurring in an extraordinary way. But I believe that coincidence is really another strong sign that energies abound around us that we mortals simply do not understand. I think the Creator has a great sense of compassion and humor, and sometimes, like a loving parent, God expresses this to us mortals by whispering—"Surprise!"

Chapter 1

Coincidences that Change the Course of One's Life

What can account for why an event takes place—a coincidence—that truly changes the course of one's life? We may perhaps find clues in seeking an answer to that question in a simple statement uttered by the great psychiatrist Carl Jung, who coined the term "synchronicity" to describe what "coincidences" are: "...the simultaneous occurrence of two meaningful, but not causally connected events..." Jung, without reservation, maintained that these were not accidents or chance happenings. He said, "Whether invited or uninvited, God is present."

Coincidences that have a major effect on one's life—saving it, or turning it in a completely different direction—give witness to a power that comes from a higher source. These are moments when the invisible world permeates the visible world. Coincidences this powerful give credence to what the noted psychologist Abraham Maslow wrote: "The great lesson from true mystics is that the sacred is in the ordinary." To quote one of these mystics, Hugh of St. Victor, "Yes, it is truly the Beloved who visits thee. But he comes invisible, hidden, incomprehensible. He comes to touch thee, not to be seen; to intimate his presence to thee, not to be understood...."

Because our earthly vision is limited and clouded, a coincidence might seem to be a trivial incident—hearing a song, meeting a child, having someone hand a Bible to you—hardly the touch of the Beloved. But if we recognize the hidden power, and can let the wonder of it fill us, then, like a curtain rising, the clouded vision clears and we get a glimpse of how truly we are connected with something, Someone magnificent, loving, and in tune with us. Even those who do not believe in a Creator/Supreme Being most often called God, cannot deny the existence of this power, which manifests itself so often as coincidence.

I have several times interviewed the Pulitzer Prize-winning author William Styron. Never was I so moved by a story of personal suffering as I was when I read his account of his tormenting depression in *Darkness Visible, A Memoir of Madness.* I interviewed him when the book came out for a feature in *The Litchfield County Times,* and was profoundly touched by his account of the "coincidence" that kept him alive.

As he related, by November of 1985, this famed novelist was reaching a crisis of internal turmoil. "I had now reached that phase of the disorder where all sense of hope had vanished, along with the idea of a futurity; my brain, in thrall to its outlaw hormones, had become less an organ of thought than an instrument registering, minute by minute, varying degrees of its own suffering...."

His physical and mental distress was so severe now that he found himself getting closer to the decision to end his life. And he explained, "I think in the popular mind, suicide is usually the work of a coward or sometimes, paradoxically, a deed of great courage, but it is neither; the torment that precipitates the act makes it often one of blind necessity."

In his book he relates how the night came, a bitterly cold one, when he knew he "could not possibly get myself through the following day." It was his darkest moment, when suicide seemed the only relief from his pain. He was sitting alone in the night, in despair, forcing himself to watch a tape of a movie. Unexpectedly, from the movie came a contralto voice singing a sudden, soaring passage from Brahms' "Alto Rhapsody."

Miraculously, the sound, he wrote, "pierced my heart like a dagger" and somehow he was able to connect with the sweetness of life, remembering "the joys the house had known; the children who had rushed through its rooms..." It was a turning point. He chose to live. The next day he was admitted to the hospital.

Why would this sudden sound of a particular piece of music have had such a profound, life-changing effect on this famed author? Certainly, it had to do with his mother. For as he writes, "my own avoidance of death may have been belated homage to my mother. I do know that in those last hours before I rescued myself, when I listened to the passage from the 'Alto Rhapsody'—which I'd heard her sing— she had been very much on my mind."

Was it only a coincidence that at the moment William Styron was close to suicide, a song his mother used to sing would play, bringing him back to choosing life? Or was it providence?

∞ ∞ ∞ ∞

While it was the miracle of a song that changed the course of William Styron's life, it was a remarkable chance encounter with a very special person that altered the direction of actress Patricia Neal's life. I had the privilege of interviewing Patricia Neal after her autobiography, *As I Am* was published in 1988. She told me how she thought, when she was young, that life would be "a miracle, so sensational." Well, much of it was, but her life was also to be traumatized by "these terrible tragedies." Her book tells of how life had not been overly kind to her—a woman rejected by the married man she loves, who buries a child, nearly loses another in a freak accident, who is afflicted by a debilitating stroke, and then faces a devastating rejection by her husband, who leaves her for a younger woman.

Her book caused a sensation because in it she tells of her affair with this married man she loved, who was, it turned out, the actor Gary Cooper. Newspapers picked up the section in her book where she told of how she became pregnant with Mr. Cooper's child and had an abortion. In her book she also tells how deeply she hurt Maria Cooper, the actor's only child, and how, surprisingly, it was Maria who led her to find a place of peace. Maria, in fact, initiated a reconciliation between herself and the actress. After Patricia's stroke, Maria, by then married to the famed pianist Byron Janis, wrote a letter to her. "I cannot describe the feeling its generous greeting imparted," wrote the actress, "and I will never forget its three most important words, 'I forgive you.'"

Yet, it was later that Maria would pop into Patricia Neal's life again, "like a miracle." The year was 1978 and the actress was doing a film, "The Passage," in France. The company was lodged in a hotel at Nice, a lovely hotel. Even though Patricia was getting expense money, her husband thought the hotel was too expensive, and "like an idiot," she writes, she went to a cheaper hotel. It was a disaster. The next day she went back to the nicer hotel, and, while she was waiting for a room, she decided to have tea in the hotel bar. Patricia writes, "something made me look up toward the door. A very beautiful young woman walked into the bar and swept the room with a glance, looking for someone. She did not see me. She turned to leave and I was drawn to my feet. I followed her to the desk and called her name. She looked at me for an eternity before she knew me, and then she gasped, 'Oh my God!'" It was Maria Cooper Janis.

They got together several times before Maria had to leave—she was accompanying her husband on a concert tour. Maria didn't know that Patricia was having severe marital problems, but, intuitively, she sensed an inner anguish in the woman who had once caused her such deep pain. She asked Patricia about her faith in God, and the actress admitted honestly that she had been struggling with belief in God ever since her stroke. Then Maria said, "I know an abbey you would love. You should go sometime."

Patricia Neal decided to check out the place Maria told her about, the Abbey of Regina Laudis in Bethlehem, Connecticut, a community of Benedictine nuns. Mother Benedict Duss, the Abbess, counseled her to walk into her pain and write her story, "insisting that I remember it all, so that I could begin to understand who I am and what I am called to do in this life," Patricia says. She did. Her coming to the abbey marked a turning point in her life and the beginning of a renewed faith in God.

Was it merely a coincidence that she and Maria Cooper Janis—with her gift of love and empathy that gave Patricia a new, life-altering direction for her life—should be in the same hotel lobby, on the same day and at the same time, in a foreign country? Or was it providence?

∽ ∽ ∽ ∽

It was seeming coincidence that altered my own life and that of a lonely boy on a cold day in November 1950. That day I walked into the post office in the small town where I lived, and I saw Sterling for the first time. That meeting was to change his life, and mine, forever.

At the time, I was a 22-year-old mother of a nine-month-old baby, Paul, and we lived in a tiny town called Cape Vincent, New York, where my former husband and I had moved to both teach school. It was the kind of tiny town that had no movie theater, no library, and no mail delivery. You had to go to the post office in person to get your mail.

On this particular day, I had baked a cake and done chores, so I went to the post office in the late afternoon, instead of in the morning as I usually did. When I walked in, I saw this child, small, dressed in ragged clothing and shoes with holes, looking like he needed a bath, a haircut, and food. I couldn't take my eyes off him. Finally, I walked over to him and asked him who he was. He answered, "Sterling." I asked him if he was hungry. He said yes. I told him I had just baked a cake and that I lived next door. If he came with me I'd give him some cake and hot chocolate. His eyes lit up.

We made some small talk as he ate. I asked him where he lived and he said his house was a few miles away. I asked him why he was in the post office and he told me he never went there, only today he went into town and got so cold he stopped at the post office to try to warm up. When my husband got home from school, we all got into the car and drove Sterling home. "Home" was a shack, with no plumbing, no electricity, no real furniture. I had never seen a place like this. I hadn't known that people lived in such misery.

I couldn't get Sterling off my mind. It turned out he was actually fifteen, and a good student. He had lived from time to time with his mother, but mostly with foster parents. I wondered what he could achieve if he were off welfare, had a decent home, and a chance for an education. I invited him back to visit and asked him if he'd like to live with us. He said yes. His mother was generously willing to let her son have a better chance for a good start in life, and so he moved in with us. Six months later we adopted him, and Sterling Bosco turned out to be one terrific son, devoted to both his mothers, to me and to his birth mother until she died a few years ago. He married Bernadette Pazera and settled near her parents in Tinley Park, Illinois, became an Illinois state police officer, and is the father of seven children. When they come to my home to visit, or I go to Illinois, I am filled with joy, remembering that sweet, blue-eyed kid in the post office, who has done, and is doing, so much good with his life.

But was it merely coincidence that I happened to walk into that post office at that particular time on that particular day? Was it coincidence that Sterling, who never went to the post office, happened to go in that day just to try to get warm? Or was it providence, opening a door, one that could give a deserving kid the chance to have a new and better life? My son and I have never doubted that God was also in the post office that day.

∽◌ ∽◌ ∽◌ ∽◌

The hand of God certainly accounted for the coincidental events that changed the life of the great Russian writer, Fyodor Dostoyevsky. He never would have lived to write his masterpieces, among them *Crime and Punishment* and *The Brothers Karamazov,* but for two life-saving and life-altering coincidences.

Born in 1821, and protected from having contact with virtually anyone outside the home by his overly strict father, a staff doctor in a Moscow hospital for the poor, young Fyodor grew up to be a recluse. In a sense his father had built a wall around his son, perhaps to protect him from what he regarded as contamination from other human beings. When at age sixteen, Fyodor entered the engineering school at Petersburg, he was regarded as a snob by teachers and classmates. He began living an interior life that he called "a world of dreams," perhaps to escape from the pain he had already seen in the suffering poor confined to the hospital garden next to the Dostoyevsky home.

While Fyodor was at school, his father left the hospital and moved to a country estate, where he became known to his employees as a cruel landowner. One day, Fyodor got the news that his father had been murdered, probably a plot by his own workers. He was traumatized. He never mentioned his father's name again, but was left with a violent inner turmoil searing his soul. Somehow, he was able to turn his anger outward, focusing it on injustice, specifically the injustice of government. He joined in meetings with radical intellectuals who wanted to overthrow the Czar in Russia and set up a republic of free people. Then, at one of the meetings, he was arrested and marched off to the Peter Paul Fortress, to await his fate.

It was the Christmas season and the air was brisk the day they put him and others into a coach headed for the Semenov Drill Grounds. The place was filled with political prisoners and troops standing at attention, ready to carry out the sentence of the military court—death to all convicted men. A priest was there, holding a crucifix, leading the doomed prisoners to a platform draped in black. Grouped in batches, they began to be led to the place of execution. Fyodor was in the third batch. He figured he had about five minutes to live.

Suddenly, as the soldiers raised their rifles, there was a loud noise as a horseman raced up to the platform. He had a message from the Czar. It was a stay of execution. The prisoners were not to be shot, but to be taken instead to an exile in Siberia. Some of the men cried out that they would rather be shot, knowing that Siberia was a punishment worst than death. But fate had interfered, and Dostoyevsky was to live.

On Christmas Eve, he was brought from the Peter Paul Fortress to the train for Siberia, and another coincidence occurred. On the sixteenth day of the journey, they reached a transit prison in Tabolsk and were detained there. Unexpectedly, several women brought dinner and clothing and copies of the Gospels. One of them pressed the holy book into his hands. The cover of the book had a slit cut in it, and, stuffed in this space, he found a note for ten rubles, enough to buy supplies and food to keep him alive in the God-forsaken place he was going. But even more powerful was the effect the holy book had on him when he began reading its messages. His turning to the Gospels, seeking to shed some light on the problem of evil, sin, and salvation, was to shape his life and his writing. He kept the book all his life and was reading it when he died.

Dostoyevsky spent four years in Siberia before he was released from hard labor. Then he was forced to serve as a soldier in Siberia, working his way up the ranks to officer before he was discharged and given his freedom. In the decades to come, he wrote classic books that bore the weight of his thoughts, creating characters, from idiots and criminals to sages and saints, in the hope of shedding light on the paradoxes of life and the relationship between us here below and our God.

In the end, by the time of his death, Dostoyevsky had shared the wisdom he learned, that in spite of pain and evil, "life is not to be scorned, and death is not to be feared." He had found an answer and could express it profoundly:

He will come—the God-man whom the world has derided as the Idiot. And they shall learn to follow him when he teaches them the true meaning of Good and Evil—that the inflictor of pain and the sufferer of pain are not two different creatures but one and the same body, one and the same soul; that each man is responsible for the action of the entire human race, and the entire human race is responsible for the action of each man. He will come, this Idiot-Savior, upon this earth where man seems real and is spectral, and God seems spectral and is real. He will come at last and teach us the one vital truth—that all men, from the highest saint to the lowest murderer, are groping by different paths towards the selfsame source of light, the light of universal *identity*, of universal *love*.

The world would have been denied the richness of Dostoyevsky's intellect and soul if he had not lived. And consider this—but for five minutes, he would have been before the firing squad, blown away, if the horseman had not arrived at that moment to stop the executions. Could that have been only a coincidence, or was it fate—providence? Then, was it merely a coincidence that a kind woman would press a Bible into this prisoner's hand as the train to Siberia made a stop? Was it a coincidence that money had been placed in the Bible, a sum that perhaps bought him some comfort in the notorious death camp to which he was being sent? Because these coincidences saved and so altered his life, they can only be construed as miracles.

ᘂ ᘂ ᘂ ᘂ

Sometimes a life-altering coincidence may seem to be a dark event, until enough time passes to be able to discern why fate played this hand. Such was the day that changed the lives of two extraordinary people who made such a mark on the world of their day and beyond—Franklin and Eleanor Roosevelt.

The coincidence that affected the dashing up-and-coming politician and led to his wife defining a new role in their relationship occurred in August 1921 at Campobello, where the Roosevelts had a summer home. They had bought a little sailboat they called the *Vireo* and had gone sailing with their boys. Suddenly, they saw great flames, and, knowing this was a forest fire, they hastened to get to the shore to help fight it. Roosevelt proved to be a valuable worker. Before four in the afternoon, the fire was out.

When the family got home, Roosevelt decided it would be a good idea to take a dip with the boys in a land-locked lake called Lake Glen Severn, on the other side of the island. After their swim, the boys went back to the house. Roosevelt took another dip, this time in the Bay of Fundy, where though it was summer, the waters were quite icy. He then ran back home. A lot of mail had come in, and the robust politician sat around in his wet suit reading it. Before long, he said he had a chill and a fever, and went to bed instead of going to supper.

Two days later, he was paralyzed. Within a few weeks, the diagnosis was in: Franklin Roosevelt had infantile paralysis, the dread disease also known as polio. This was years before it would be discovered that a virus caused polio, so there were neither preventive measures nor cures at that time.

It appeared that Franklin's career was over, and it would have been, except for his wife. She would not consider him an invalid. Early on she made him crawl to get him moving on his own, and she later got him to use crutches. She took over as father as well as mother to her sons, learning to pitch a tent, paddle a canoe, and mount a horse. With the encouragement of a friend, Louis Howe, who had worked with Franklin when he was Assistant Secretary of the Navy a few years earlier, Eleanor did all she could to keep Franklin interested in and in contact with politics. To accomplish this, Mr. Howe urged her to get into political work herself. She did. She started with the Women's Trade Union League, and where she went from there— leaving her mark as a woman who had a passion for human equality and peace—is history. As for Franklin, he made history as the President who carried the burden of World War II, and, for the first time ever for an American President, was elected to four terms. His last term was never finished, interrupted by his death on April 12, 1945.

Some historians have called the coincidence of the Roosevelts being in their boat near where a fire erupted the "turning point" in FDR's career, meaning it had set him back from the bright political career track he was already on. More likely, the fire was the turning point for Eleanor. If Franklin hadn't gone to fight the fire, would he have needed, or wanted, to take a swim in the waters that turned out to be unseasonably icy? If he hadn't become paralyzed and had zoomed along in his career, would Eleanor have remained behind the scenes, content to maintain the expected role of mother and wife? If so, we would never have heard her voice, which spoke so forcefully to the conscience of the world, urging all to abolish poverty, seek racial equality, provide for the education, health, and welfare of women and children everywhere, open new homelands for refugees, and make peace the foremost goal of all nations so that the world would be united and human.

We can't set limits on the possibilities that can be activated by unseen forces. We can only be open to accepting that a greater power may be the mover when an apparent coincidence affects the course of a life. The coincidence of the fire at Campobello in 1921 led to life-altering events for the Roosevelts—and indirectly prepared them both for a destiny they could not have imagined, but would courageously embrace.

○∕○ ○∕○ ○∕○ ○∕○

Like the Roosevelts, hit with a sudden tragedy out of their control, I too knew the shattering effects of a tragedy that put my life on hold, until a coincidence led me back to the light. This was a life-altering coincidence, so immediately and directly an answer to prayer that I couldn't possibly doubt that Someone with significant power and a lot of love was listening. In 1994, I needed some heavy duty help to get me out of a life-draining, emotional slump that had been brought on by the dual loss of my children—my son Peter by suicide, and my son John and his wife Nancy by murder. On the surface I looked fine and was functioning well. But I knew I was constantly falling back into mourning, and I didn't want my life to be stuck in that place.

In late January of that year, I went to Florida for a week's vacation to begin preparing for the third anniversary of Peter's death, which was coming up on March 18. I spent a good deal of my time there reading a book on the origins of Christian spirituality. The more I read, the more I felt drawn to wanting to experience the place where Jesus' story unfolded, where his message was first heard.

When I got back home, I told my kids that I really wanted to go to the Holy Land, to walk where Jesus walked. Of course, that was a pipe dream. I didn't have the time or the money to do that.

That was a Saturday. On Monday I went back to work, and that morning I got a phone call from an acquaintance who works for the Ministry of Tourism in Israel. She said, "Toni, get ready to go to the Holy Land."

I nearly fell off my chair. Was she some kind of psychic mind reader? She went on to tell me that a historic conference of Christian and Jewish religious and academic leaders from around the world, the first ever, was going to take place in Jerusalem the first week of February. Would I like to go, include a tour of the Holy Land, and write about this in my syndicated column for *Catholic News Service?* "Tanya, are you offering me a free trip to the Holy Land?" I asked. She said yes. I gasped, and said yes myself.

I knew this had to be more than a chance happening. The hand of God was clearly involved. I went to Jerusalem, had a fabulous, joyful experience at the conference, seeing so many old wounds healed between Christians and Jews, and wrote many stories upon my return.

But there was much more. On the tour that was included with the five-day trip, our bus driver took us to the Western Wall, which used to be called the Wailing Wall, the last remnant of the destroyed Temple courtyard and the holiest shrine for the Jewish people. I walked to the side of the wall where the women prayed and felt inspired as I saw so many young Jewish women reading their prayers from Hebrew prayerbooks. Many of them at the wall were placing their hands on the stones.

I decided to pray as they did, and so I walked to the wall and raised my arms putting the palms of my hands on the stones. I thought of the mothers down through the centuries who had prayed at this wall for their dead sons, and suddenly I started to cry like I had never cried before. The tears were like a fountain. I felt as if I were a part of a pietà that endured throughout history. The tears just flowed, but they weren't my tears alone. I was joined with all the Rachels crying for their children throughout history, and as I cried with them, the loneliness was flushed out of me. It was a welcome catharsis.

I learned then that it was the loneliness of my pain that had kept me locked in mourning. Now I knew I was not alone in this searing loss of children. I had touched and been touched by two centuries of mothers, and in sharing our pain, I lost the loneliness and ended the mourning.

We receive many signs that God loves us. For me, one of those signs was a phone call from a friend that made possible a deep desire of mine and led to an enormous healing. I didn't know then why I felt such a strong desire to go to the Holy Land. But I think it was a God-force moving me to look to where I would find the place that held healing for me. As for the phone call itself, which came just two days after I had told my children about my desire to go to the Holy Land— well, there's no way this could be relegated to chance.

I came back and my life was changed, altered for the better. I did not mourn Peter on the third anniversary of his death. I celebrated his life.

ᏇᏇ ᏇᏇ ᏇᏇ ᏇᏇ

More than we may realize, there are very profound reasons why some persons experience a coincidence that sets their lives in a new direction, heightening their consciousness and prompting them to take on work that will have a lasting impact. One such person was a priest, Bartolomé de Las Casas, a sixteenth-century aristocratically born Spaniard who became a principal figure in early American history. A coincidence so moved him that it shaped his life's work and gave him a noble characterization that would be forever his: "the Great Apostle of the Indies."

Las Casas came to the West Indies in 1502, when he was twenty-eight years old, at first working as a soldier and a merchant before turning to the priesthood. He is thought to be the first person in America ordained to the priesthood, which occurred in 1512 or 1513. At this time, the natives of these lands were slaves of their conquerors and treated with deplorable cruelty. They could be worked to death because their lives were worthless in the view of their captors. Because Las Casas had taken part in the bloody conquest of Cuba, he was given an allotment of Indian serfs as an award. He thus became a slave owner, and apparently saw no harm in this. He was not like the others, however, for his treatment of his slaves was gentle and just, and they loved him.

But once clothed with the robes of priesthood, Las Casas began to see the world differently. He could no longer be indifferent to what he saw going on all around him—the brutal treatment of the Indians. But what could one person do? Then, on the eve of Pentecost, 1514, he happened to pick up his Bible and open it at random. His eyes fell on the page before him. He stared at the words of the thirty-fourth chapter of Sirach and they struck him like lightning: "The Most High is not pleased with the offerings of the wicked; neither is he pacified for sin by the multitude of sacrifices. The bread of the needy is their life; he that defraudeth him thereof is a man of blood. He that taketh away his neighbor's living slayeth him; and he that defraudeth the laborer of his hire is a shedder of blood."

The power of those words seared the soul of Las Casas, and from that moment he knew that the system of slavery was wrong, and that he had a mandate from God to try to abolish this evil. He returned his serfs to the governor, and, knowing he had to get approval in Spain if the Indians were ever to get better treatment, he went back to that country to plead his cause. Las Casas was forty at this time. He lived to be ninety-two, and never did he stop in his mission to free the Indian slaves. He became the historian of the truth about what the conquerors had done in America. His masterpiece, *Historias de las Indias,* exposed the sins of domination, oppression, and injustice inflicted upon the native people of the west after they were "discovered" by the Europeans. He was the noblest of men in his love for the poor and the wrongly afflicted, far ahead of his times in seeking to expose and end the cultural injustice of the conquering European powers that had taken control of Latin America. His writing on the injustice of slavery applied then and now to slavery anywhere.

Could it have been only by coincidence that his Bible opened to that particular verse on that evening before Pentecost? And was it a coincidence that this would occur just before Pentecost, which is the feast celebrating the coming of the Holy Spirit, who was promised to bring wisdom and courage to the apostles—precisely so that they would have the conviction and the guts to bring Christ's message of justice and love to the world? Certainly, one could surmise that the

Holy Spirit infused Las Casas that night, setting him on a new life course that would be his destiny.

Most likely the random opening of the Bible by Las Casas was not haphazardly initiated at all. The judgment of history would have to affirm that a higher power was at work here, guiding the hand of this priest to open the book, to see words that would arouse his soul and launch him into the work so sorely needed in that place and time. Miraculously, the random opening of a Bible, in effect, opened the door of this man's heart, immediately and forever redesigning his life, permanently altering how he would live from that day on.

Chapter 2

Coincidences that Reveal How Lives Spiral around Other Lives

Many a time I have encountered stories that illustrate in a remarkable way that we are not isolated islands, but connected family members. When this happens, from some place deep in my subconscious I hear again words that challenged me long ago when I first read them—"God has created me to do some definite service; God has committed some work to me which has not been committed to another. I have my mission. I may never know it in this life, but I shall be told it in the next. I am a link in a chain, a bond of connection between persons...."

These are the words of the great British churchman, John Henry Newman, later a Cardinal of the Roman Catholic Church. I have meditated often on what these words mean, and I have come to see many examples in my life and in the lives of others, present and past, that highlight just how surely "we are links in a chain." Yet, I think we fail to focus on just how these connections occur and what they mean. If our consciousness could be raised to see what the eyes miss—that certain elements, which will somehow affect two people, are put together and set in motion by a benevolent force—then doors of understanding would be opened. We would comprehend that something beyond ourselves has set the scene for us to be linked to another, creating a chain, causing a connection that empowers, enhances, or embraces both. If we never open our eyes—and maybe our minds and hearts—we will never grasp the power of these chains, we will only call them "coincidences."

In May of 1991, I had the privilege of interviewing a psychiatrist, Dr. Stephen Herman, for a Father's Day feature for *The Litchfield County Times*. I had read a book he had written about child custody, called *Parent vs. Parent,* and thought it was the best I had yet read on the subject. A month or so after this, I wrote an op-ed piece on coincidences, and, to my happy surprise, Dr. Herman sent me a letter telling me a story of a coincidence that had happened to him. He began:

Back in 1978, an article appeared in *Medical World News* about a brave medical student at Downstate Medical Center [in Brooklyn], who was on a dialysis machine three days a week but who still kept up with her classes. This woman was extraordinary and, although quite ill, kept pace with the other students and dreamed of becoming a doctor. I was very moved by the article.

A few weeks later, a physician wrote a letter-to-the-editor blasting Downstate for accepting this student, complaining that she was taking up space that ought to have gone to a healthy medical student, attacking the student and the school for wasting taxpayer money, etc.

I was furious. I wrote to the letter-writing Texas doctor, blasting him for playing God. I can't remember what else I wrote, but rest assured it was on the same theme. I then copied that letter and mailed it along with a supportive one to the medical student at Downstate. I never heard from either party.

Now, it's 1987. I've decided to write a book on child custody and I'm working with a freelance editor who is helping me with the sample chapter for my book proposal. She has lunch one day with an editor at Pantheon and tells her about me and the book idea. The Pantheon editor asks my name. When the freelance editor tells her, she just about swallows her tongue.

The Pantheon editor, Sarah, now relates a story. Seems that back in 1978, *Medical World News* ran a story about her sister, a medical student at Downstate and on dialysis. The article was followed by a nasty letter from a physician. Her sister became very depressed and hopeless. When she received my letter, she improved, with spirits lifted, and I, apparently, became a family hero. Sarah told her lunch companion that she had been trying to find me for about ten years!

Sarah, the Pantheon editor, called me. She sent me a copy of my letter to her sister, which the family had always kept.

I then met Sarah for dinner. Through tears, she told me her sister rallied for a while, but she could not go on fighting her illness. Transplants hadn't worked. Dialysis made her ill. She committed suicide before she ever became a physician.

Sarah and I had, as you can imagine, a most emotional dinner. She asked me about my book idea. She said she liked it. I said, with some discomfort, she wouldn't publish my book just because I had written the letter. Absolutely not, she said. The idea was a good one and would stand on its own.

We secured "the deal" with a hug instead of a handshake, and *Parent vs. Parent* was conceived. Of course, I had a contract, but the real contact was in the hug and what came before.

A coincidence? Maybe. But somehow this agnostic, cynical, scientific, medical doctor thinks otherwise. We all touch each other in different ways. *Lives spiral around lives.* And maybe, as you have said, as rich as this is, it's all just the beginning.

When I read that letter, I was struck by his insight that "lives spiral around lives" and I began to focus on this. More and more I would hear stories that told of chance encounters or unusual meetings that brought two people together in a way that made a major impact on their lives. It opened up for me a whole new dimension of how "coincidences" often have a connecting principle. These incidents of lives spiraling around lives may not always be of a life-altering magnitude, but, truly, they add a richness to those who encounter each other for the better in unexpected ways.

Take, for example, this story from the life of the great Polish pianist—and patriot—Ignacy Jan Paderewski. In 1894, the thirty-four-year-old acclaimed virtuoso was on a concert tour from east to west in

America. While he was touring the western states, a couple of enthusiastic Stanford college students persuaded Paderewski to perform. They guaranteed him two thousand dollars and the pianist agreed.

Imagine their embarrassment when, after the concert, they found the receipts would not cover the agreed-upon fee. They went to Paderewski with their dilemma, and nervously awaited his reaction. Pretending to be very serious, and reminding them that people should always meet their responsibilities, the maestro then went on to suggest a practical way out of the problem. They were to pay all their expenses, deduct a percentage for their own labor, and give him what was left.

You can imagine how touched these young men must have been with this meeting with Paderewski and his lesson that justice should always be tempered with mercy. And certainly, the pianist gained two friends.

What he didn't know then was that one of these young men, a geology student named Herbert Hoover, would one day repay him more than he could imagine, by helping starving millions in Paderewski's own country of Poland.

It was Hoover, raised as a Quaker and one day to be president, who became the organizer and supervisor of the massive European relief operations during and after World War I that saved millions of lives. He had a large presence in postwar Poland, and had become a friend of Paderewski, who worked so tirelessly for his country and its people. Because of his powerful position, Hoover pressured the socialist Jozef Pilsudski to appoint Paderewski as premier in the government. He regarded these two men as "two out of the six or seven great idealists of the world," and with these appointments, the United States became the first nation to recognize the new postwar Polish state.

This was 1920, twenty-six years after Hoover had met the great pianist at Stanford. If he and his friend had made the two thousand dollars promised to Paderewski, would they have had an opportunity to learn firsthand what a noble person he was? Maybe not. Maybe they would have shaken hands and said good night, and Paderewski might have been remembered as a fine pianist, but not as a kind and other-centered person. Because of this almost random meeting, the lives of Hoover and Paderewski were ultimately and forever joined. Was it coincidence, or fate, that caused these two lives to spiral in a way that brought honor to both of them?

∽ ∽ ∽ ∽

I have witnessed one story of how two people were linked that could never be relegated to chance. It is about my brother and his doctor.

The story goes back to when I was eleven years old and we lived in Albany, New York. At the time, my parents rented the top floor of one of those typical three-story city houses, joined by mutual walls on both sides and forming rows of brick buildings, like cutouts or clones, on both sides of the long streets. There was one "flat," as the apartments were then called, under us and another in the basement.

The owners, Mr. and Mrs. Lizzi, lived in the basement. They were a lovely older Italian couple with a few grown children. One of their sons had recently married a beautiful young woman newly arrived from Italy, and he and his wife lived in the middle flat. My job that summer was to take care of my little brother Joey, then three years old. He mostly loved to ride his tricycle up and down the sidewalk, and many times I was fiercely bored. One thing that helped a lot was being able to spend some time with my young neighbor on the second floor, now a happy mother-to-be.

They called her "Catuzza," which meant, my father told me, "sweet little Catherine." The "-uzza" was a diminutive that Italians put at the end of a name when a child was particularly sweet and it usually stuck until adulthood. Catuzza was indeed sweet, and I loved to be near her.

By summer, Catuzza was well into her pregnancy and lonely since her husband, a shoemaker, worked long hours to provide for his budding family. She knew very little English, so I would help her learn and Joey would put in his two cents worth. He had golden curls, and she would twine these around her fingers. Her smile would always make me feel that she was wondering about her own child in her womb.

Sometimes when the baby would kick, she would let me touch her stomach, and once, when Joey was close by, he too put his hand on her stomach, feeling the baby kick. I told him that was her baby moving inside her, and Joey kind of glowed with fascination. Catuzza was embarrassed. In those days children weren't supposed to know about babies being in a mother's tummy.

At summer's end, we moved, and I lost track of Catuzza. My brother Joe Oppedisano grew up to join the U.S. Army, go to college, establish a career with the New York State Labor Department—and contract a fatal illness at age thirty-five. I shall never forget the day I was restless at the university where I was working on Long Island in late 1972. I kept thinking of my family in Albany all day and finally at 4 P.M. I picked up the phone and called my sister Rosemary. "How did you know?" she asked me. "How did I know what?" I answered.

She told me—that day my brother Joe had been in surgery since early morning as the doctors removed a swollen spleen. Considering the degree of malignancy, they didn't want to take bets on how long he would live. Sometime after that, when I visited Joe, he told me that he had had this strange experience. He "saw" the inside of his body and all through him were little bristles, like those on a brush.

This didn't make much sense until the lab reports were all back and Joe's doctor gave him the news. He had a fatal disease called Hairy Cell Leukemia, and the doctor, to explain to him what this meant, showed him what Joe had already "seen" in his strange and unexplainable visualization—"hairy" cells under the microscope.

Now commenced the battle, and Joe, with the family's intense support, was determined to live. There was one strong ray of hope—in the doctor he eventually found, a hematologist named Dr. Frank Lizzi, most respected at St. Peter's Hospital in Albany.

That was a familiar name to me and one day when I was visiting Joe in the hospital, I told him that when he was a tot, we had lived in a house on Irving Street where our landlord was named Lizzi. Joe was aware of that. In fact, he said, our one-time landlord was the late grandfather of his Dr. Lizzi. It was like a light went on. Was Dr. Lizzi's father a shoemaker, and his mother named Catuzza? Yes, said Joe.

They were Dr. Lizzi's parents. When he told me that his doctor was only three years younger than himself. I gasped. It hit me how remarkable it was—that Catuzza's baby, yet unborn, was to be the doctor who would save Joe's life.

At that moment, Dr. Lizzi came in. When he put his hands on Joe, what I saw then was not two men, doctor and patient. I saw a golden haired child with his hand on the tummy of a blushing mother-to-be, and I marveled at the mystery of connections.

Never would anyone have been able to imagine that the unborn child would one day himself return that touch, bringing the miracle of life with it. Who put the pieces in place that would forever link the lives of these two men? That's the question that rattles the mind of a truth seeker.

ᧄᧄ ᧄᧄ ᧄᧄ ᧄᧄ

The chains of coincidence that we experience sometimes appear to be responses to signals that we ourselves are unconsciously releasing. Everyone can tell a story of a time when they were thinking of a specific person, and at that moment, or shortly after, that person appears down the block or in the office, or the phone rings and it's his or her voice. At times like these, it is not difficult to believe that we are capable of communicating on another level of consciousness. If we could but tune in to the nonphysical energies being constantly generated through our physical bodies, isn't it possible that we would then be able to expand our communications into as yet unheard of dimensions? The connections that we relegate to simple coincidences may be visible clues that we should wake up and consider those possibilities.

One of my favorite personal "chains of coincidence" stories begins with a frustration. My brother Joe had lent me a book he said I would find fascinating. It was called *Cosmic Consciousness, A Study in the Evolution of the Human Mind*, written by a pioneer psychiatrist named Richard Maurice Bucke and published originally in 1901. I loved the book and its stories of people throughout history who had experienced illuminating mystical experiences. Among these incredible people was the American poet Walt Whitman. Dr. Bucke had spent much time with Whitman and, in addition to including him in this book, had also written an impressive biography of this poet.

After I returned the book to Joe, I felt like something was missing in my life. I desperately wanted a copy of it for myself. I started checking bookstores. No luck. I contacted the publisher who had put out the edition my brother had. No luck. It seemed as if, at that time, the book was out of print and nowhere easily to be found. So constant was my verbal wish that I could find a copy of this book that my kids started to tease me that I was sending messages out to the universe. I responded, probably nastily, that I wished the universe would then respond! Meanwhile, I had read a story about a modern composer putting some of Whitman's "Leaves of Grass" to music, and with that timely hook, I had written a story about Walt Whitman for *The Litchfield County Times*.

A few days later, I got a wonderful affirming letter about my Whitman piece from a woman named Florence Rome Garrett. She told me it was her family who had been the publishers of Walt Whitman's work and she was delighted that someone cared enough to write about this fine man. I wrote back thanking her and saying I would love to meet her one day.

Not long after that, I got a call at the office from Barrie Kavasch, a lovely woman I had gotten to know because of her work with Native Americans and the books she had written on the foods of the American Indians. She asked me if I would like to go with her to visit a friend, a woman she knew I would just love. Would you believe— Florence Rome Garrett! I said "yes, what an amazing coincidence," and we took the trip, about an hour and a half's drive, a few days later.

Barrie was right. I loved Florence, who was also a poet. She showed me some first editions of Whitman, and one poem-in-progress in his handwriting, with scratched-out words and corrections. Among her books, was the biography of Whitman by Dr. Bucke. I just had to ask Florence if she knew where I could get a copy of *Cosmic Consciousness*. She knew the book well, but didn't know where to find one. When we left, we all knew this had been a very special visit.

A few days later, I got a call from Florence. She had found *Cosmic Consciousness*. It was in a bookstore with mega-shelves of books, owned by a passionate lover of books, in a town called Easthampton, Connecticut. I sent him a check. He sent me the book, a hardcover edition put out by University Books in 1961. I was delighted.

Could all this have been a random chain of circumstances? I don't think so. I think I had sent my request out on wires we can't see. Somehow my plea for Dr. Bucke's book was being heard and answered via Walt Whitman, Barrie Kavasch, and Florence Rome Garrett. We became links in a chain that would lead me to gain the gift I was intensely seeking.

ॐ ॐ ॐ ॐ

Back in the mid-fifties, I was in my early twenties with a couple of children and just getting going as a writer. I was back in my home-town of Albany, and one of my former college professors, who was now superintendent of schools, asked me to teach creative writing in the adult education program. I had about twenty students—and I was the youngest in the class. The only one close to my age was Ruth Cotich, an Australian married to Peter, an American, and a mother of very young children, like myself.

Ruth and I hit it off immediately. She would bring in samples of her writing and I knew she had talent. I loved working with her because of her enthusiasm. I taught the class for two years, before having to move to follow my then-husband to a new job on Long Island. My pride and joy was Ruth, who, in that short time, as a beginning writer, sold several of her stories to prestigious teen maga-zines, like *Ingenue* and *Seventeen*. We pledged to stay in touch, and did, at least every Christmas ever after. A couple of times we talked by phone, and when Ruth wrote a book for teens, I happily did a book review recommending her fine work.

Fast forward to 1994. The first edition of my book, *Finding Peace*

Through Pain had just come out, with the title *The Pummeled Heart*. I was doing book signings and other promotional work. The manager of a Barnes & Noble in North Haven, Connecticut, booked me in late fall for a 3 P.M. Saturday signing, and I traveled the distance to be there. Chairs were set up, and the place was very quiet as it got to 3 P.M. Then the manager told me the bad news. Somehow the newspaper ad had come out saying I was doing the signing at Waldenbooks, not Barnes & Noble. I shrugged. That's life.

Just then a woman came in accompanied by a youngish couple. She came right up to me and said, "Toni—I'm Ruth Cotich." I gasped. I hadn't seen her in nearly forty years! From her last Christmas card, I knew she had moved to Florida. But what was she doing this day in North Haven, Connecticut?

She told me that her husband had died, and they had buried Peter back in Albany. However, her daughter—the younger woman with her—lived in Connecticut and she decided to visit her on her way back to Florida. When she was talking by phone to her daughter, Ruth asked her if there was a bookstore nearby because she wanted to get this new book written by her friend Toni Bosco. Her daughter called Barnes & Noble, and, to her surprise, the manager said they not only had the book, they had the author—she would be here on Saturday to sign copies. Ruth couldn't believe her good fortune. Nor could I believe mine.

The best was that here I was, with no one showing up because the ad had gotten fouled up, which meant I had plenty of time to give to Ruth. She had a couple of hours to spend before her daughter had to pick her up, and we spent that time together, rejoicing in the good fortune of being reunited after all these years.

Could it be only by coincidence that the ad got bungled? I doubt it. I think my life was meant to spiral with Ruth's for mutual enrichment. We have been separated by distance, but that alone.

∽ ∽ ∽ ∽

Thomas Dermody, editor of *The Catholic Post* in Peoria, Illinois, who responded with enthusiasm when I wrote one of my syndicated columns on coincidences a few years ago, sent me a letter telling what he had recently experienced:

I was out for a noon walk in downtown Peoria. As I was passing a school for delinquent and troubled youths, a thirteen-year-old girl bolted from the building, crossed an interstate highway and disappeared into downtown. Soon representatives from the home came out looking for her. They were anxious, I would later find out, because this girl had twice previously tried to commit suicide. The group returned without finding the girl, whose name I was told was Sarah.

Antoinette, as I continued walking downtown, I had the feeling that I would play a role in this episode. I stopped at the downtown Catholic church, lit a candle for Sarah, and offered my eyes to God if I could be of help. I walked around downtown for about ten minutes, and was returning back to our newspaper offices when I saw Sarah crossing the street right ahead of me!

I prayed for words, for I knew nothing about this girl or her situation, and called her name. She asked if I was a cop. I said no, and asked if I could walk with her. To my surprise, she said yes. We ended up walking and talking for an hour and a half. Eventually, we wound up at the home of a friend of hers. She went inside. I called the children's home. She was returned to what I can only hope is a caring environment.

I can't help but believe that God had a hand in getting me, at just the right time, near the door from which Sarah bolted. I had decided very late in the lunch hour to go for a walk in the first place. And perhaps the bigger God-incident is that God brought our paths back together in a big and busy downtown.

Nobody can know for sure why Sarah's and Tom's lives touched this day, but one life spiraled around the other on that downtown street that afternoon—perhaps so Sarah could be saved.

Tom Dermody isn't alone in being fascinated by these so-called "coincidence" stories. Just say to someone that you had a strange, a funny, a great, a peculiar, an unforgettable—or whatever—coincidence just happen, and they'll be urging you to tell them all about it. Who wants to know about coincidences? Just about everybody.

∞ ∞ ∞ ∞

Chains of coincidence can sometimes occur in ways that have a life-enhancing dimension. A person can be at a moment of despair, from a financial crisis or an emotional trauma, and suddenly and unexpectedly, help comes almost out of nowhere, from someone who at some time was linked to them. A believer in spiritual forces would not have a hard time seeing this kind of help as having a divine hand in it, even though it is being carried out in a very human way. A nonbeliever—unable to comprehend that people who become links in a chain are bonded in ways that defy ordinary physical or scientific explanations—would call this a mere coincidence.

And could it be that some people have been created to do such a spectacular work that a force one might call divine energy is the power behind the help that is given to them? Consider the case of Nathaniel Hawthorne, nineteenth-century New England author of such famed books as *The Scarlet Letter* and *The House of the Seven Gables,* and who is considered one of the greatest fiction writers in American literature.

This brilliant but introspective man seemed to be plagued by bad luck, brought on perhaps by his own genius, which made him prefer "to dream of life, instead of living it," to use his words. Perhaps this was because of his childhood losses: his father died at sea, a tragedy that turned his mother into a recluse, who also forced her three children to be shut off from the world. At age seventeen, however, Hawthorne entered Bowdoin College, and there he became friends with two fellow students whose lives would be linked with his: Henry Wadsworth Longfellow, who would become the foremost poet of his day, and Franklin Pierce, destined to become president.

Hawthorne had a rocky career, holding such odd jobs as a weigher of coal in the Boston Common House, while writing stories that indicated his brilliance, but brought in very little money. Things were a little better financially for him and his wife Sophia after James Polk, a Democrat, was elected president, and Hawthorne, a staunch party supporter, was appointed a Surveyor of Customs at Salem. But his luck failed four years later when Zachary Taylor won the presidential election, and Hawthorne was dismissed from the custom house.

Now, pitifully poor, Hawthorne, in a strange coincidence, received a considerable check from a man named George Hilliard, along with a touching letter saying that this money was "a debt of gratitude for what you have done for American literature." It turns out that his college friend Henry Longfellow was behind this. At this time, the poet headed a group of intellectuals at Harvard, and he communicated his belief in his friend Hawthorne to them. These fine men literally kept the wolf away from Hawthorne's door.

The other friend did not forget him either. After his election as President, Franklin Pierce appointed Hawthorne to the American consulship at Liverpool, England, a position which at least for a few years brought Hawthorne a heightened status and financial security. The bond of connection between these two friends was truly lifelong. Franklin Pierce was with Hawthorne when the famed writer died.

The chains forged in his college days that linked Hawthorne with two friends became a lifeline, in effect, that helped make it possible for him to write the classic books that will endure forever. But maybe there was another power at work, stimulating a quiet call to his friends to remember Hawthorne, to ensure that the great writer would produce the work he had been put on earth to do. Cardinal Newman affirmed, "He does nothing in vain. He knows what He is about."

ॐ ॐ ॐ ॐ

Another story about the spiraling of lives involving students at the same college is that of lyricist Tom Jones and composer Harvey

Schmidt, who set musical theater records with their production, *The Fantasticks,* which still holds the crown for being the world's longest running musical.

They met at the University of Texas when Tom was an acting student who switched to directing, and Harvey was an art major with no musical training, but who wanted to compose. Somehow they got together and did a musical review called *Hipsy Boo!* About all this taught them was that they really could "collaborate," Tom Jones once told me in an interview.

Well, this was 1950. From college, both of them were suddenly in uniform, sent right into the midst of the Korean conflict. When they got out of the service and both settled in New York, their paths crossed again. Harvey became a very successful commercial artist and Tom struggled to become established as a play director. Meanwhile, they followed their souls, collaborating, trying to produce a great musical. They discovered a play by Edmund Rostand called *Les Romanesques,* where two fathers invent a feud in order to make their son and daughter fall in love. They had found their story; Tom found he could write impressive lyrics, and Harvey found he really was a composer! In 1960, their achievement opened as *The Fantasticks* at the Sullivan Street Playhouse in Greenwich Village in New York, exactly ten years after their first "collaboration," *Hipsy Boo!* as college students in Texas.

The spiraling of their lives continued, with other praised musicals coming from their collaboration—including *110 in the Shade; I Do, I Do; Celebration;* and *Philomen.*

If these two talented men hadn't met, would they have pursued their dream, which brought delight to so many audiences? Who knows?

∽ ∽ ∽ ∽

Sometimes initial encounters between two people bring them together in a way that will make a major impact on one or both of them. An unexpected chain of circumstances begins that brings a change for the better in their lives, that truly adds richness. The story of how I came to teach a journalism class not long ago, and met a student named Kevin Canfield, is a case in point.

In early September 1994, I got a call from an administrator at the Torrington campus of the University of Connecticut asking me if I would teach a one-semester beginners journalism class, starting in a week and a half. The man who was supposed to teach the course had to take a temporary leave because of illness in his family, he explained, and someone recommended that the college call me. I was still executive editor of *The Litchfield County Times,* putting in long hours, and, in addition, had committed myself to give a number of talks on my newest book. I needed another commitment like the proverbial hole in the head. And a week-and-a-half preparation time wasn't exactly enticing. But about a dozen students, who needed the course and the credits, would get shut out if the campus didn't find a teacher. Reluctant as I was, how could I say no?

It turned out to be a great class with terrific students, some of whom wrote well enough to get a column or two published in the course of the semester. One of these students was Kevin. He was a quiet, serious, sensitive young man of twenty-four, married and a father of a three-year-old daughter. He was close to halfway through college studies and on his way to getting a degree. He knew that he wanted a profession, that he didn't want to get stuck indefinitely doing the landscape work he now did to help support his family. I liked this bright, courteous, and responsible young man.

At the beginning of the next semester, I got a call from Kevin, asking me if I would be his mentor for a course he was taking that allowed him the freedom to choose a specific field of work. I agreed, and Kevin came faithfully to my home every week for the semester. We focused on writing and Kevin worked hard, showing talent and meeting deadlines. He promised to continue practicing his writing. I believed he would.

That summer Kevin again called me. He wondered if I thought he was ready for an internship at a newspaper. I asked him some tough questions, prepping him for what internship would entail, mainly a lot of work for little or no money. He convinced me he was ready, willing, and able. By "coincidence" I had kept in touch with a young woman who had once been a fledgling reporter under my editorship and who now was an editor for the daily newspaper in—guess where?—Kevin's home city! I called Pat Daddona, and she said that it just so happened that the *Register Citizen* was looking for a good intern. My recommendation helped. Kevin got the job. A few weeks later, he was offered a salaried position as a reporter. He's doing a terrific job now with *The Hartford Courant.* Am I ever proud!

The chain of coincidences began with the teacher dropping out, my getting a call to fill in, Kevin signing up for the class, Kevin finding the confidence to call me and ask me to be his mentor, my having kept in touch with Pat, her paper needing an intern at just this time, and Kevin showing enough skill to be offered a job as a reporter. Was all of this set into motion because it was time for Kevin's life to change course? I believe that there is a connecting principle in these apparent chains of coincidences that brings a bonus of riches to those who encounter each other in these unexpected ways.

৵৹ ৵৹ ৵৹ ৵৹

If ever there was a life story that shows how strangely chains of coincidences connect people over time and distance, it is the odyssey of a Connecticut man named Joseph Sanady. A soft-spoken man with a sense of humor, Sanady was born in Hungary in 1916, reaching his young manhood in the turbulent years of World War II. Just before the outbreak of the war, he had become a young soldier in Hungary. He was in uniform when his country was compelled by the Nazis to become a German satellite or face an occupation.

In November 1943, he was commanding a platoon of men outside Soviet Kiev as the Red Army was counterattacking. Unexpectedly, a conscript labor brigade of Hungarian Jews under separate command, ordered to retreat to Budapest, wandered into Sanady's camp. His attention became riveted on one of the men, not only because he seemed educated and gentle, but also because he didn't have a coat and he was shivering from the cold. Vehemently opposed to the Nazi anti-Semitism, Sanady waited for an unguarded moment and then shoved his own khaki overcoat and emergency rations into the surprised man's grasp. Neither of them said a word, so as to avoid any attention, and the next day the Jewish laborers were gone.

Months passed, and Sanady was sent back to Budapest to become part of the city's defense against the impending Soviet invasion. One day an important visitor walked into his office. His name was Dr. Julius Kovesdi and he was an assistant vice consul of the Swedish consulate then under the authority of the famed Raoul Wallenberg. He looked familiar, but it took a while for Sanady to really recognize him. Kovesdi was the man to whom Sanady had given his overcoat on the freezing day outside Kiev! Though Kovesdi was a Hungarian Jew, he'd been granted Swedish citizenship and diplomatic immunity.

Kovesdi came to say thank you, telling Sanady he had searched diligently for his benefactor. But he also wanted to offer him a refuge in the Swedish consulate, knowing that when the Soviets captured Budapest, the Hungarian officer would be shot or sent to Siberia.

Sanady thanked him, but said no, he would stay firm in his duty as a soldier. And then, in a twist of fate, their lives crossed again. Sanady learned of a plot to get Kovesdi arrested and shot while off the Swedish embassy grounds, during one of the last roundups of Budapest Jews. He got word immediately to Kovesdi and saved him. Budapest fell in January 1945; Sanady was packed in a cattle car and sent to Siberia, where he was a prisoner until 1947.

Oddly enough, Sanady and Kovesdi both ended up in the United States, Sanady on the East Coast and Kovesdi on the West Coast. With busy lives, they had little contact until 1973, when fate again put them in touch. This time it was Sanady who needed help, when an anguished son called him from California to say he was nearly killed by drug dealers. The only man Sanady knew to call for help on the west coast was Dr. Julius Kovesdi. He who had been saved by Sanady twice in the war years, now lost no time in getting his benefactor's son the help he needed.

Sanady and Kovesdi were two men, linked together in war and

peace by something stronger than blood—a spirit that rose above the earthly boundaries of position. They were joined by grace to be partners in extraordinary, life-giving moments. The chain that began with one man handing another a coat and provisions that would save his life, extended to another time, another place, where those linked by this chain would again be agents for saving a life. These men illustrate in a special way the words of Cardinal Newman, that God commits a special work to each person on earth. And help comes to each to be able to do that special task, sometimes in ways we can only describe as coincidence.

∞ ∞ ∞ ∞

In my own experience, the late Richard Guilderson's life spiraled around mine in a way that brought me to the field of journalism and the work that has become more a mission than a career. I first met Dick Guilderson back in 1956, when he was the advertising manager for *The Evangelist,* the weekly paper of the Albany diocese. In the previous year, I had moved back with my then husband and five children. I saw an article in *The Evangelist* saying that Dick, who believed there should be more communication in the church, had begun a Diocesan Communications Arts Guild. At that time, I had already been writing a lot of articles and stories for various magazines and this looked like a story to me.

I called Dick at *The Evangelist* and he was quite willing to be interviewed. I got to meet him and his family and sit in on some of his early meetings. I then wrote the story, which was published in a Catholic magazine. We kept in touch now and then for the next few years, but, as continually happened ever since I got married, my husband lost his job and we had to move yet again. This time we landed on Long Island, in the Diocese of Rockville Centre, which had recently been split from the Brooklyn Diocese.

In early 1962, I was reading *Newsday* and saw where the Rockville Centre Diocese was going to get its own diocesan newspaper, to be called *The Long Island Catholic,* and was to be edited by Msgr. Richard

Hanley. I had to look twice when I saw the name of the assistant editor—Richard Guilderson. Before the day was over I sat down and wrote him a congratulations letter, but I couldn't mail it until the next day. Coincidentally, that next morning I got a phone call from Dick. Thinking that he wanted to let me know about his new job, I started congratulating him, telling him I now didn't have to send the letter. He wasn't calling to tell me that, he said, and then asked, "Guess who's going to be our women's editor?" I was stunned. "Not me," I said. "I've got five little kids, and I don't know anything about journalism."

Dick laughed and said, "Yeah, but you know a lot about writing." I countered that I was tired of writing and I had decided to give it up. Dick convinced me that I should "just come in and meet the Monsignor."

Well, a few days later I borrowed a neighbor's car and drove the forty miles from Smithtown, where I lived, to Rockville Centre, where the paper would be published. I met the two Richards at a restaurant, walked in, sat down, and very nicely said, "If you ask me to do dress patterns and recipes, I'm walking out." The two of them looked at each other, smiled, and Msgr. Hanley started to talk, fast. Later I learned that they called him "machine-gun Hanley" because of the way he fired out words. When I got back to my car I realized he had given me five assignments. I did the work, and while I don't remember actually accepting the job, I worked there for the next eleven years. It was a few years later that I also learned why the two men had laughed at my first pronouncement. It seems that just before I walked in, Msgr. Hanley, a Vatican II-era priest, had said to Dick Guilderson, "If she walks in and wants to do dress patterns and recipes, I'll throw her out."

In the late sixties, Dick Guilderson left *The Long Island Catholic* to go to Washington, D.C., to work for the national Catholic News Service. A few years later he developed terminal cancer and left that office. But again our lives spiraled. Catholic News Service was looking for a Catholic woman columnist, and people there, having heard about me from Dick, got the idea that I could do the job. I got a call on September 18, 1974, which happened to be my birthday, offering me the position. I was honored and accepted, and I have continued as a columnist for CNS ever since.

Dick Guilderson died shortly after that, at the age of forty-nine, the exact age Msgr. Hanley was when he died a few years earlier. I got to visit him and his family in Maryland where they lived. We talked about how our lives had spiraled, and together gave thanks for the gifts God had helped us give one another. A final coincidence—Dick told me on that last visit that he wanted to write a book about all he had learned from pain. Neither of us knew then that—after the searing pain of losing two sons—I would be the one to write that book, *The Pummeled Heart: Finding Peace Through Pain* (Twenty-Third Publications), a work which has led me to a new mission of helping people suffering from the trauma of loss.

If it hadn't been for that phone call from Dick Guilderson in March of '62, I might never have stayed with writing, and I certainly would not be in the healing ministry that has resulted from my being a writer. Does God have a plan for each of us? I am absolutely certain this is true, and that God uses people to help us discover and follow that plan.

∞ ∞ ∞ ∞

Another case in point about God having a plan for each of us could be the story of Hollywood and television actor, James Douglas. Jim became something of a household name and face from twelve years of soap opera performances in *Peyton Place* and *As the World Turns*. But his story began much earlier than that, when he had acted in Hollywood films and in television shows, like *Dragnet, Father Knows Best, The Donna Reed Show,* and many others.

"I was in *G.I. Blues* with Elvis. I played his buddy. In *A Thunder of Drums,* with Richard Boone, Charles Bronson, Richard Chamberlain, and George Hamilton, I went riding into the sunset and got killed. In *Sweet Bird of Youth,* with Paul Newman, I was the bartender," he recollected.

At this time, he and his wife Dawn had become friends with a beautiful young star named Dolores Hart. Jim had met Dolores by chance at Fox Studios where she was under contract with Hal Wallis. A convert to the Catholic faith, Dolores was happy to be able to spend some time with a solid family, as she saw the Douglases and their three children to be. There weren't too many like them in Hollywood, she said. And then Dolores had the opportunity to go to New York to do a Broadway play, *The Pleasure of His Company,* with Cyril Ritchard. George Peppard, also in the play, was leaving, and "Dolores called me, asking me to come out and read for the part. I didn't get the role, but I stayed two weeks in New York. It was my first encounter with the East. It was March and snowing, and I was real blue," he said, understandably, having to deal with yet another "bad break" in the acting business.

It was at this time, too, that the young actress, also feeling a kind of void, first visited the Benedictine Abbey of Regina Laudis in Bethlehem, Connecticut, that would, surprisingly, figure crucially in both their destinies. For, as Jim told me, his heart was putting him on a search for greater meaning and purpose in life as the years were going on, and this subsequently put him and his wife on the road to the Abbey as well. For this change in direction, he credits Dolores Hart, who left Hollywood and Broadway in 1963, "at the height of her career," to respond to a different call that changed her life. She entered the Abbey and has been faithful to her call ever since.

As Jim Douglas continues his story, "*Peyton Place* lasted for five years, and after that run as Stephen Cord, I was offered the lead in *Bracken's World.* But by now the draw to the East was there. We often visited Dolores—now Mother Dolores—and little by little, we were moving our way toward the Abbey." Again, it appeared that coincidence, or fate, was having a hand in his career path. "If I had taken that lead [in *Bracken's World*], I would have lasted in it about a year and a half. Instead, moving to New York, I was offered the role of Grant Coleman in *As the World Turns* and stayed with the show seven years."

It was during these years that the Douglas family moved to

Connecticut, to be closer to their friend Mother Dolores and the Abbey. "I had my Catholic faith, but there was a lot I didn't know about it," said Mr. Douglas, who revealed he "reestablished myself with the church when I came to Regina Laudis in 1974." He and Dawn, also an actress, became Benedictine Oblates (laypeople who have made a covenant with the nuns to serve as "an outreach of the Abbey").

Sadly, Dawn, beloved by everyone who knew her, died in May of 1996. Jim still acts, directs productions, and writes. But you find him every morning at Mass at the monastery church of the Abbey of Regina Laudis. As for what he has learned from the Benedictine tradition that has so shaped his life, he answers, "Otherness—having a focus outside myself."

The story of how the lives of Dolores Hart and James and Dawn Douglas spiraled around each other—from Jim's bumping into a starlet at a Hollywood studio to their decades of working together, following God's call—has all the elements of a Hollywood script. But I think the script came from another place, a Higher Source, guiding three people together to use their impressive talents for acting in becoming a force of goodness for the benefit of so many others. Lives do spiral around lives, and perhaps it is not fantasy to believe that a knowing Director is designing the action.

Chapter 3

Remarkable and Unexplainable Incidents that Defy Ordinary Rules

More and more I find myself marveling at the stories people tell me of surprising happenings that have them baffled, yet pleased—and changed. Almost always, they say, that no matter how disbelieving they may have been about other-worldly forces at work in their lives, a "coincidence" they experienced that defied ordinary rules has convinced them that more is going on here than we can yet explain.

My friend Gloria K. was one of these storytellers. She's a health professional who has worked with young-to-old people, anyone with a physical disability and little money. A few years ago one of her patients was a thirty-year-old woman, confined to a wheelchair, an unwed mother with a preschool child. The father, George, had a severe drug problem and couldn't work enough to support himself, let alone contribute to the family. Gloria had a hard time dealing with George, an utterly charming man who could easily deceive people with his phony sincerity and pretend lovableness. But she was on to him right away and told him outright that he needed to search his soul, ask God's forgiveness, and straighten out his life.

Fast forward to another of Gloria's patients, an elderly

woman. She really wanted something this one day and asked Gloria to get it for her—a Bible. She said she wanted to read again the Twenty-Third Psalm, perhaps in preparation for what she perceived to be the coming end of her life. Since Gloria's mother is a religious, churchgoing woman, she figured her mom might have an extra Bible around the house. In fact, she did, a slightly worn one, which she gave to Gloria.

That night Gloria opened the Bible, she knows not why, and noticed some writing on the inside cover. There, in a boy's handwriting was—would you believe—George's name, an address, and the name of a school for religious education.

The next day Gloria visited George. She handed him the Bible and asked if he had ever seen that book before. His face went white. He was in shock. It was his Bible from years back. He began to cry as memories from an innocent age flowed back. Gloria told him to keep the Bible, not as a closed book, but as a living message.

When Gloria told me this incredible story, we speculated on how that Bible could have been in her mother's house. Her mom couldn't recall how she got the Bible, but thought it might have been at a used bookstore somewhere. Gloria's scenario was different. She felt that somehow God arranged that her mother would pick up this book and keep it until the right moment came to return it to its owner. Coincidence—or was this the Lord working again in mysterious ways?

ௐ ௐ ௐ ௐ

The dictionary uses two expressions to explain coincidences, "striking occurrence" and "mere chance." But when these happen to us, we have to ask, "Is that all there is to it?" For few of us can dismiss what Carl Jung called "synchronistic phenomenon" so casually. How many times has something like this happened to you: you're thinking of someone, the phone rings, and it is that person on the phone? One night I was reading a newsletter from the State University of New York at Stony Brook, where I had worked for nine years, and saw an article about a dear, longtime friend, Jane Porcino, and a program she had done on gerontology in China. Jane and I had worked together at the university in the seventies, but I hadn't seen her or heard from her in quite some time. I was delighted to read news of her. As I was reading about her, and looking at her photo that accompanied the article, my phone rang. It was Jane! We made plans to get together to renew our memories and catch up on our lives. I would wager that everyone reading this can remember a time when something similar happened to them.

∞ ∞ ∞ ∞

I had long wanted a medal of the saint who is honored on my birthday, September 18, a seventeenth-century Franciscan, St. Joseph of Cupertino. He was a sweet young man, but he was considered by his mother and the townspeople to be something of an imbecile. His widowed mother treated him as though he were a nuisance because he was slow to learn, couldn't keep a job, and was distracted and forgetful. He embarrassed her. Actually, young Joseph was a classic loser. He apprenticed to a shoemaker, but couldn't make it. He entered the Capuchin monastery as a lay brother, but kept dropping plates and never learned to light a fire. The Capuchins had to let him go. Eventually, his uncle, a Franciscan priest, got Joseph admitted as a novice. He worked in the stables and seemed to have a gift for talking to the animals. But that only convinced everyone that he was a dummy, and it seemed he would never make it to ordination. But when it came time to be tested, miraculously he was asked to repeat the one Bible passage he knew and understood, and so he was ordained. In the early sixties, a fine movie was made about him called *The Reluctant Saint,* starring Maximillian Schell and Ricardo Montalban.

As Joseph became ever more holy in his life, according to first-hand accounts, he began levitating as he prayed, and for this reason the Roman Catholic Church, in canonizing him, declared him the patron saint of pilots and air travelers.

I had not had any success in finding a medal of my patron saint, but I always felt one day I would. Now, as it happens, my oldest son

Paul—proprietor of a gallery in the Manhattan Arts and Antiques Center in New York—has long been a dealer in coins and medals. Each December he participates in the annual International Coin Show, always held in a big New York hotel. I have often gone to help him for this show, staying at his apartment. Paul wasn't the greatest housekeeper and, being enormously busy both before and during the show, his place was a colossal mess, but I coped.

In December 1991, we had finished the Saturday show and had gone to his apartment. I wanted to sit on his couch, but he had thrown papers, coins, and medals on it. I had to be extra careful that I wouldn't cause damage. Very gingerly, I put my hands down first before I sat. Then I felt something under my right palm. Clearly it was a large medal. Curiously, I picked it up to see what it was. Would you believe that it was a medal of St. Joseph of Cupertino! I shouted to Paul, asking him where he had gotten this medal. He said it had come in that week along with a bunch of other medals he had ordered. Did I know that saint? he asked. When I told him how I had been looking for years for such a medal, he said, "Good. It's yours."

Was it only by accident that a medal of St. Joseph of Cupertino would be included in a cache of saleable historic medals? Considering all the coins and medals on the couch that night, I could have touched dozens of medals that would have had no meaning for me. Yet, my hand covered the only one that would touch me. Was it part of a grander plan that I was to find this medal at long last? I like to believe that it was this, and not mere chance, that gave me that gift.

⚬⚬⚬ ⚬⚬⚬ ⚬⚬⚬ ⚬⚬⚬

Talk to anybody and they can tell you about coincidences that make them smile or feel good. Consider the following stories:

Chuck Vrtacek, a musician/writer I have worked with, told me that when he was writing a piece once on assignment for a newspaper about the French musician Erik Satie, he had the radio on. "Whose music should suddenly come on the radio? Yes, Satie's. Not only that, they played a number of selections, enough music to last until I had finished writing the piece. Then I had to make a phone call and was put on hold. Guess what music came over the phone? Satie's 'Gymnopedie!' I think he's watching me...."

A dear friend, psychologist Penny Russianoff, who played in the movie *An Unmarried Woman* with actress Jill Clayburgh, was widowed a few years ago when her husband, noted clarinet teacher Leon Russianoff, died. I knew that she and Leon were a deeply devoted couple. Shortly after Leon died, Penny had to drive from New York to Connecticut. She grabbed a tape from a table full of tapes to have something to play in her car. It was, she said, "a potpourri of jazz that Leon had put together."

She was listening to the selections, when abruptly the music stopped, and there was Leon, talking to her, telling her that this is a tape of "my beloved wife's favorite jazz pieces. This is for you, Penny, because you've made my life so wonderful. These pieces are dedicated to a great lady. I love you, Penny."

My friend told me in relating this surprising experience, "I could have picked up any one of two hundred tapes. I just happened to pick up this one. It was one he made more than ten years ago. I think it was a direct message for me from Leon."

Was this just a chance happening? Or was there another force that guided Penny's hand as she picked up a tape? Certainly, hearing Leon's voice, so clear, "exactly as if he were talking to me today," brought great joy to Penny.

Then there was a letter I got from a reader, Marilyn, from Kentucky. She told me she was a recovering alcoholic who drank at home, "and more so, when I cooked." One night she was cooking, and craving a drink so badly that she heard herself cry out to God— "I don't want to drink. Help me in some way. Show me you hear me!" At that moment, "the phone rang. It was someone from our church prayer chain." This was the intervention she needed to get control over her craving.

"This was not a coincidence," she wrote me, "but definitely a God-incidence. And one I shall never forget. To me it was awesome and shows God does hear our prayers." It's not often that prayers get so instantly answered. Was she right? Was this a God-incident?

This is a story sent to me from Dr. Joseph Evers of McLean, Virginia. His office is about a mile and a half from a Catholic church, and when time permits he likes to go to the church for some quiet prayer. One particular spring day, the sky was overcast and rain was in the air. He didn't have his car that day, and he had no rain gear, but he decided to put the matter of the weather into the hands of the Lord and walk to church.

During his twenty-minute walk, no rain fell. Inside, he prayed, feeling, he wrote, "very peaceful." Then, rather suddenly, the storm came, and he could hear the pounding of the rain. Somehow he didn't worry about how he was going to get back to his office in the downpour. He started down the aisle "in sort of waitful anticipation." Then, as he approached the foyer of the church, he saw a disposal can, and there, sticking right up the middle of it was an old umbrella. The maintenance man, standing beside the disposal can, had just cleaned out the foyer closet. When Dr. Evers asked if he could take the umbrella, the man answered, "Help yourself."

The physician ended his letter to me, saying, "Like Gene Kelly in that old movie, I was 'singing in the rain,' all the way back to the office. Coincidence? I don't think so, do you?" No, I don't think the umbrella was there by chance, either, but rather by design.

A touching story was sent to me by Linda Smith, a single mother in Massachusetts. Her six-year-old son needed new sneakers, but she didn't have the money to buy him a pair. It happened that Dottie, a friend from her church, asked her to go with her to run some neighborly errands. When they were finished, they went to Dottie's house for a bite to eat. To Linda's surprise, her friend went into her son's room and walked out carrying a pair of sneakers, exactly the size her son needed. Dottie said she had bought these for her own son some time ago, but he never wore them because he didn't like them.

Linda writes, "I had not told Dottie of my son's need for a pair of sneakers, and I cried while telling her this, and how I had asked Jesus to provide sneakers for my son. She was also touched because she said very often she had thought of getting rid of those sneakers, but something stopped her. Now she knew that Jesus had a need for those sneakers." And Linda concludes, "There might be some people who would say 'merely coincidence,' but I know better."

For this mother, the gift of a pair of sneakers that brought happiness to her young son was truly a miracle in disguise.

০৯০ ০৯০ ০৯০ ০৯০

Certainly one could say it was a "little thing," on the face of it that happened to Mert McMichael of Missouri. But for her it was life-changing. I'll let her tell her story:

My brother and I, at the same time, were diagnosed with cancer. His percentage of survival was higher than mine but in six months he died. I was devastated by his death and feared for myself. Counseling and drug therapy had little effect. My life was a nightmare.

One evening my husband insisted we join friends for dinner. To my surprise, they brought another couple along. I halfway listened to table conversation while fighting back tears, for life had become a constant battle with fear. The stranger was talking about his years of drinking and the long road back to sobriety. He talked of the card he carried with AA's twelve steps for getting back freedom from the alcohol. He explained the power of the steps. I thought, I'm not an alcoholic, but a fear-oholic. Hope stirred deep inside me. If only I had the card. Suddenly I felt a total surrendering to God, as a prayer whispered across my soul—"God, I am powerless against fear and my life is wasting away. Please place the card in my hand and I will know you are with me, giving strength to overcome the bondage of fear."

I spoke to no one about my desperate need for the card.

The next day, I reluctantly went to a resort area to look at land for sale. The place was depressing, almost deserted except for people showing the property. Returning to the car, hot and tired, I hurriedly tried to get the children into the backseat, when my two-year-old bent down and picked up something from the pavement. Instantly, I grabbed it from his hand. It was dirty and I scolded the child for picking it up. Suddenly my eyes focused on the words. It was the little card—The Twelve Steps Back!

That was sixteen years ago and my life has never been the same since my close encounter with God.

ॐ ॐ ॐ ॐ

I'll never forget the phone conversation I had with a woman from Colorado in the early months of 1996. I had gotten a letter from Ann (she asked that I not use her full name) that broke me up. She had been very dear friends with my son John from twenty years back, but had lost track of him for the past four or five years, after each had married and gone separate ways. She had only just found out that John and his wife Nancy had been murdered two and a half years earlier in the home they had purchased in Montana. How she found out about this was, she said, an amazing coincidence.

I had written an article about the deaths of my two sons and my daughter-in-law for *Woman's Day* magazine, and it had been published under the title of "Heart and Soul" in the November 21, 1995 issue. It was illustrated with a photo of me sitting next to the wall in my bedroom where I have the high school graduation photos of my six birth children and the Navy photo of my adopted son, Sterling. Ann had seen this article a few months after it had been published, and suffering shock at realizing the John Bosco in the story was her longtime, beloved friend, she wrote to me, sending the letter to *Woman's Day* and asking them to forward it to me. They did, and when I received it, I immediately phoned her.

It was a conversation that was hard on both of us. Ann, a classical pianist, had had several sad losses in the previous year, including the deaths of a favorite friend, Marilyn, a pianist like herself, from cancer and a friend, Richard, who had choked to death while eating at his desk. Adding to her troubles, her marriage had failed, and her dog, too, had suddenly collapsed and died. She told me that in her mourning, she had touched the walnut kitchen island that John—who was a professional cabinet/furniture maker—had built for her and thought how distressing it was for her to have lost contact with him. John became increasingly on her mind, but she knew he had moved from Colorado and so she didn't try to contact him.

Knowing she was in a troubled state from the losses she had suffered, her parents came for Christmas. They had brought "a huge stack of magazines for me. After they departed, I was feeling unwell, exhausted, too tired to do a thing. I saw the magazines and grabbed one, looking for escapism and relaxation. I started thumbing through. Then I saw the photo—the wall of photographs. I immediately recognized John's photo. That photo was the first one he had given me. He told me when he gave it to me that it was old and he really didn't like it but it was all he had."

Ann kept thinking it couldn't be John. It must be another Bosco, "another similar-looking Italian." But the two girls in the photos were named Mary and Margaret, his sisters' names. "I tried to think, what was his mother's name? He'd so wanted me to meet her. And then I just screamed, 'Oh Jesus, not my John!'"

We spent a lot of time talking, and we tried to console each other. While Ann was in real pain over the tragic news, she knew it was right for her to have found out about John's death so that she could mourn him properly. Oddly enough, her mother had never read that issue of *Woman's Day* or she would have recognized John since she had met him when he lived in Boulder. "I *never* would have seen the magazine article if she hadn't brought it," Ann told me.

We have kept in touch ever since. I think John would have wanted Ann to know he is now in God's heaven, and he would have wanted us to be in touch to help strengthen one another. Perhaps it was only a coincidence that Ann would be reading a magazine she absolutely never would have seen but for the fact that her mother had left it. And what are the odds that it would be the magazine containing the only article I had written about the deaths of my sons? A coincidence? I have a hard time believing that.

∞ ∞ ∞ ∞

My longtime friend, Frank Bianco, a writer like myself, told me an amazing story that defies explanation. It is about a Trappist brother he met when he was doing research for his memorable book about this famed religious order, *Voices of Silence* (Anchor/Doubleday). Brother M. had been in the monastery twelve years, but, acknowledging that he was gay, had left. He became an interior decorator on Long Island and for twenty years ran a very successful business. During this time, he had also left the church.

On a day that happened to be Ash Wednesday, he arrived to pick up draperies and other materials from a woman who was his principal supplier. She stared at him and then told him, "There's nothing on your forehead." He bristled and said, "So what?" She answered, "You were a Trappist. You should be close to God. Let me tell you, if you have no place for God, I have no place for you." And with that, she refused to give him the materials he desperately needed to fill his orders.

He went home, plunged into depression, and began to think. About nine that evening, he left his home and started to drive aimlessly. He somehow ended up on a road, where he came upon a Catholic church. He pulled up and to his surprise saw a man and a woman standing there. They beckoned him to come into the church with them. He followed them. They went in and up to the altar. He could hardly believe it when a priest came out and put ashes on their foreheads, just the three of them. Brother M. broke down, crying. The priest said, "Come talk to me." They talked until four in the morning. When he got home, Brother M. reached for the phone and called the Abbey of Gethsemene. "I want to come back," he said. And he returned.

That was more than a dozen years ago, but there's more to the story. When Brother M. returned to thank the woman for helping him open his heart, she didn't know what he was talking about. She didn't remember a thing about Ash Wednesday. As for the priest, "he remembers nothing of that night, either," said Frank.

I ponder this story, wondering what really happened. Could it be that Brother M. encountered heavenly visitors, leading him to the church and the altar? I can hardly imagine that a priest would be in church on Ash Wednesday night to give ashes to three people. I doubt if there's an earthly explanation for the events of that day, but one thing is certain—God's grace was there in abundance.

೦ৎಂ ೦ৎಂ ೦ৎಂ ೦ৎಂ

Another story from Chuck Vrtacek is one that defies explanation. He lived with his fiancée Cindy and her daughters in a house they rented from her ex-husband's mother. "The place is one hundred and fifty years old and at various times we have both seen what appears to be a figure moving around a corner or through a doorway. It seems we only catch a glimpse of it. The most curious and verifiable experience we've had involves an old dictionary. This is one of those twenty-five-pound Webster's dictionaries, the kind libraries have. As I'm sure you know, these books are heavy and their pages very thin."

Chuck related that at one point there was a question about whether or not they would be allowed to stay in this house, since Cindy's divorce had been finalized. Spring was approaching and they had been talking about the garden they wanted to have. So they decided to pray one night, asking the Holy Spirit for help in letting them stay in the house. In the morning, they noticed something strange about the dictionary which was on a table in a hallway. "There were five slips of paper sticking out from the edge of the dictionary. They were precisely aligned, as if someone had opened the book and carefully arranged each slip before closing it. The slips of paper were all in the handwriting of the girls' great-grandmother and had to do with gardening. There was a pencil sketch of a garden on one and other notes [about gardening] on the other pieces of paper," Chuck told me.

"We took it as an omen [or answer to prayer] to go ahead and plant the garden and so we did just that. Obviously we were able to stay in the house. We still believe it's because we were wanted here."

A person could speculate that the papers had been in the dictionary all along, but what would explain the fact that they "emerged" the morning after Chuck and Cindy's prayer?

જ્જી જ્જી જ્જી જ્જી

One could claim that all of these true stories are evidence that miracles abound all around us, if we but tap into the fact that we are spirit as much as we are body. As Dr. Paul Pearsall writes in his astounding book, *Making Miracles,* we can "participate in the making of our own miracles." He explains, "Unfortunately, the word *miracle* has gotten a lot of bad press. It has come to mean that God intervenes in the operation of this world and breaks his own rules by causing something grand to happen that 'can't happen.'" Dr. Pearsall, who twice was near death and records the personal miracles in his life, has a new vision. "Miracle making," he writes, "is a common human trait that grows from the spark of divinity shared by all of us." And what energizes us so that we can join forces with God and others is, in one word, love.

Dr. Pearsall's life-support system was wife, family, and friends: "My connection with them kept me connected to something more powerful than my illness. Their love became a force that carries me through the worst times of my life. Love created a source of energy that was so real that many of the medical people who cared for me reported actually seeing and feeling that energy and its powerful impact on my survival."

In all the stories just related, love was a vibrant reality. When love is energized, miracles can happen, even though to some these miracles may seem to be only coincidence.

Chapter 4

Coincidences that Bring Help in Times of Need

Stories abound about people who have been caught in a situation of danger, or found themselves in circumstances that could leave them vulnerable to harm, when, unexpectedly, help came. Such stories about how help came suddenly and surprisingly truly bear the mark of the fingerprints of God.

I always remember an incident from the life of St. John Bosco (1815-88), our family patron saint and founder of the Salesians, which I used to tell in story form to my children. This remarkable man from Turin, who spent his life rescuing outcast boys in Italy, founding places that could be called "boys' towns of Italy," had incurred the wrath of businessmen. That's because he took the boys off the streets and taught them a decent and practical way to earn a living so they would not be exploited as day laborers for a pittance by the rich. These men didn't like to have their profits reduced.

It so happened that Don Bosco, as he was called, used to walk alone at night, often through dark alleys, to find the homeless boys and to offer them help and hope. But this was a dangerous practice, because robbers and murderers were known to lurk in the Turin alleys. The priest never worried about himself, however. He had important work to do and he would never let fear stop him.

One night, as he was beginning his long walk back to the home, he heard footsteps that seemed to get closer from behind him and then suddenly saw another man rushing toward him. The two pounced on him, one throwing a cloak over his head. Clearly they had murder on their minds, no doubt they were paid assassins hired to get rid of the troublesome priest. Don Bosco, a powerful man, was on the ground, struggling to free himself, when he heard a low, menacing growl. Before the men could move the priest, a huge gray dog leaped at them. Both of them fell to the ground, yelling, "Don Bosco, call off your dog!" He answered, "Take this cloak off my head." At that, the dog walked a few steps away and stood still. The would-be murderers obeyed. Don Bosco then asked them if he had their word that they would do him no more harm. They promised, and off they ran.

The big dog had been still as he watched Don Bosco brush some dirt off his clothes. Then the priest told the dog to come home with him and he'd give him a good supper. And, oh yes, he thanked the dog for coming in the nick of time to save him. The dog seemed to understand and walked alongside Don Bosco to his home. He opened the door and motioned to the dog to come in, but, as he crossed the threshold and turned again, the dog was gone. The next day, Don Bosco asked his boys if any of them had seen this dog. From his description, it would have been impossible for the boys not to have seen a dog that size, but none had.

Don Bosco was puzzled, too, as he thought about this dog that he immediately named Grigio, which is the Italian for gray.

Could it have been only a coincidence that just at the moment when Don Bosco would surely have been killed, a strange, huge dog appeared, terrifying the would-be murderers? Or was it, rather, that God had much work ahead to be done by this remarkable priest, and so gave him a hand to keep him safe?

As the Don Bosco story continues, it was said that every time after that first incident, when the priest would go on a dangerous mission, the gray dog was waiting to go with him, staying close until Don Bosco was safely home. Then Grigio would disappear again. This went on until Don Bosco earned the respect of all and it was safe for him to go on his errands of mercy without needing protection. Then Grigio showed up one last time, as if to say good-bye to this holy man.

ֆֆ ֆֆ ֆֆ ֆֆ

My son-in-law Rick Van Valkenburg called me not long ago to tell me about an experience he had had that day, one in which he became the agent for protecting a person from harm. He and my daughter Mary, with their seven-year-old daughter Sophia, live in Manhattan. Sophia's school is quite a distance from their apartment, and she has to be brought to school and picked up each day by one of her parents. On this particular day Rick was on his way to pick up Sophia, but he went a way he never goes, on an avenue he is never on. He had chosen to go this way because a grocery store on the block had advertised some specials and he thought he'd stop in and buy some things.

As he was crossing the street, he noticed a man in a wheelchair, with a man next to him who seemed to be pushing the chair around. The man in the wheelchair appeared to be an invalid from muscular dystrophy or a similar illness because his arms were frozen across his chest. He looked to be trying to manipulate the wheelchair with his feet.

As Rick got closer, he realized the standing man was actually harassing the disabled man. He decided to see if he could be of help. When he got to the wheelchair, the man looked up at him and, in a pleading way, asked him to help. Rick, who is an impressive, strong six-foot-four, stepped in. The man who was tormenting the disabled man, taunted him and snarled. Rick, taking a chance that this man didn't have a hidden weapon and evil on his mind, told him to get lost, and then pushed the wheelchair across the street. He took the man, who was frightened but grateful and relieved, to his home.

As Rick told me later, but for the coincidence of his deciding to walk on that avenue where he never treads, on that day at that particular time, who knows what damage the miserable harasser might have done to this disabled man. As Rick put it, it appears that the

Lord puts things into motion so that at the moment of need, good can be done and evil averted.

ॐ ॐ ॐ ॐ

The very next day, I was talking on the phone to a woman who reads my column and has become a phone friend, Kathleen Broderick of Massachusetts. She told me how she and her husband had gone to Friendly's with their two grandchildren for ice cream and soda on a late Sunday evening. A couple with a baby were sitting behind them and they could overhear that they were having a problem. It turned out that they both walked out of the restaurant at the same time, and they found out what the problem was. Car trouble.

Kathleen and her husband asked if they could help and the couple explained that they lived in the next state and, while they had called their family for help, it would take a couple of hours for someone to get there. It was very cold out and so Kathleen invited them to come to their home to wait. They all had a grand time and at 11:30 P.M. they went back to the parking lot.

A few minutes later, a car pulled up with the young woman's brother and father. When they all heard the story, the father smiled. He said that all through the long drive, he kept praying that his kids would find a nice family to take care of them until they got there. What a coincidence that the Brodericks were in the same place at the same time! Prayers do get answered, he said.

Kathleen simply commented that this was no coincidence. "We were meant to be there, to help keep this young family safe."

ॐ ॐ ॐ ॐ

Anna Lahrman's story also illustrates how a coincidence is sometimes a life-saver. In the case of this St. Louis, Missouri, mother, the life-saving part is literal. The story begins when her son Louis, who was twenty-three, went canoeing with some friends on a Sunday. That evening when he got home he complained that his back was hurting him. He mentioned that the canoe had tipped and he was thrown into the water. His mother concluded that he had twisted his back.

In the morning, however, he had so much pain, his father took him to the emergency room of the local hospital. The doctor said, given the canoe story, it sounded like Louis had pulled a muscle. He gave him a prescription for a pain killer and told him to stay in bed for a week. But the pain seemed to get worse, and the next day Anna found her son crying. She prayed to the Lord to help her suffering son. Still, she trusted he would feel better by the end of a week, because the doctor had said so.

Now shortly before this apparent injury, Louis had met a young woman named Cindy, a nurse, and they had gone out on a couple of casual dates. To Anna's surprise, on the third day, Cindy came to see Louis, who was by then very depressed. Anna left the two alone to talk, but before a half hour was up, Cindy came downstairs and said she was taking Louis to the hospital. "I don't like what I see," she said. Louis' brother Michael was home and he and Cindy managed to get Louis into the car. At the hospital, the examining doctor ordered x-rays and a spinal test. They made a startling discovery. Louis had an abscess on his spinal cord that had ruptured. The infection had already spread to his lower back area, and he was operated on immediately.

The doctor who did the operation on Louis told Anna, "Mrs. Lahrman, your son is one lucky guy. Had you waited just a few more days to bring him to the hospital, and if we hadn't operated, your son would have had permanent damage to his spinal cord. He would have been paralyzed from his waist down. He would have been in a wheelchair all his life."

As Anna told me, "My thoughts were of Cindy. She was the one who got Louis to the hospital, not me. When Louis came home from the hospital, he never went out with Cindy again. Maybe she saw him as a patient, not a boyfriend, and he saw her as a nurse, not a girlfriend."

But that doesn't surprise Anna, for she sees Cindy's presence as having had another purpose. "When my son needed help, I prayed to God, and God sent a nurse right at the exact time of Louis' need. I will always have a special spot in my heart for Cindy. You can call the surprise of her showing up at the house a coincidence, I call it a miracle—God's answer to a pleading mother's prayer."

∞ ∞ ∞ ∞

I remember reading a story in *Guideposts* magazine (March 1989) that caught my attention because it was written by a woman from Danbury, Connecticut, a town about three miles from where I live. It was by Nancy Martin and told of a harrowing experience she had on a December night when she had gone Christmas shopping.

What happened to her is the terrifying fear many women have—she was in a parking lot, and somehow a man forced his way into her car. Nancy thought she was going to die. The man kept telling her, "Get down or I'll kill you." She tried to move away from him, roll down the window, and call for help, but he punched her so hard that she was winded and helpless for a moment. And so, as the car sped away, she called on the only one who could help her—Jesus. She prayed, asking him to help her. "Jesus...you are my only hope," she said aloud.

Somehow she found the courage to yank on the steering wheel and honk the horn. The car veered, and the intruder hit the brakes. He tried to go on, but mysteriously, the brakes had locked. On top of that, the horn had stuck. The man was enraged and Nancy thought he might kill her. She just kept repeating, "Lord, Jesus, save me." He told her to get out of the car. She responded that the door was stuck and he was the one who would have to leave. Incredibly, he threw open the door and ran off.

With the horn blaring, people were coming from all over to help. As soon as she could move, Nancy swung over into the driver's seat. She touched the horn, and it stopped blaring! She touched the brakes and they unlocked! "Somehow I was not surprised," she wrote, "I had relied on the name of Jesus."

Is it possible that the horn blasting and the brakes locking at that moment were just coincidences? Perhaps someone without faith in

God might say that. But the fact is that a woman was protected from impending evil by a force that was unseen but clearly felt.

∞ ∞ ∞ ∞

A little child was in mortal danger one summer about twenty-five years ago—and Amy Clinch of East Falmouth, Massachusetts, has never forgotten that day.

She, her husband John, their son David, and John's parents were together on vacation on Cape Cod. On this particular day, after breakfast John drove to a public laundry to wash their clothes. While the laundry was being done, he drove down an unfamiliar road and found a beautiful beach in a remote area. Since his parents were leaving for home that day, John and Amy had invited them for lunch, thereby delaying their usual early morning beach visit. Because John was so impressed with the beach he had discovered, after his parents left he suggested that he and Amy and David go there for a change.

They had barely arrived and were about to sit near the water's edge when a woman ran toward them screaming, "Is there a doctor or nurse here?" She was pointing to a man carrying a small boy from the ocean. Amy is a registered nurse, and at that time had been recently trained in cardiopulmonary resuscitation. Instinctively she took over, calling for a blanket and starting CPR. John called for emergency medical help. For what seemed an eternity, there was no response from the boy. Then he started to move, spitting up sea water and finally opening his eyes. Amy continued CPR for about twenty minutes, until the arrival of an emergency medical team. They rushed the boy to the nearest medical center for observation and treatment. Later, Amy and John heard that the boy had recovered.

"Over the years, we have discussed the events of that day," Amy wrote. "Everything seemed to fall into place." Then she enumerated, "One, we had never been to that beach before and have never gone since. Two, we never go to the beach that late in the day. Three, we were close to the water because John had promised David he could dig for clams. And four, I had recently completed the CPR course. Put all these things together and I think it was more than coincidental."

Without a doubt, God used the Clinch family that day to save and protect a child from fatal harm.

∞ ∞ ∞ ∞

A young woman would have been fair game for trouble on an early evening when she was stuck at a gas station somewhere in southern Indiana if it hadn't been for a man from Westport, Massachusetts.

Don McCarthy had been traveling from Chicago to Kentucky and stopped to get gas. It was getting dark and as he filled his tank, he noticed a young woman, about eighteen, who seemed very distraught. He asked her what the problem was, and she said she had a flat tire and couldn't change it. She was on her way to Kentucky, too, having recently moved there with her mother and stepfather. She had asked the two men working at the gas station to help her, but they said they didn't have time to change her tire. Perhaps their strategy was to wait until she became really desperate and then offer to help at a bloated price.

Don McCarthy sensed the young woman's vulnerability, completely unprotected in a strange place with night coming on. And so he went over and changed her tire. She was very grateful. "I told her that if my wife or daughter were in a similar situation, I would hope that someone would be there to help them," Don wrote me.

Then something funny occurred. Don asked her where she was from before her recent move to Kentucky, and she told him Brockton, Massachusetts, the town next door to his own!

Don feels maybe we're not as vulnerable as we think. Maybe we have an invisible friend who's always there, who comes from and is a part of God and shows up when we are in the greatest need. For that young woman, that invisible friend who showed up seemingly by coincidence, turned out to be an almost former neighbor named Don McCarthy.

∞ ∞ ∞ ∞

"All nurses have patients they remember clearly through the years," writes Bernadette "Bunnie" Anderson in her moving book, *My Father's Will, Out of Grief into Faith,* which gives an account of her many years working to help heal the people of Papua, New Guinea. One touching story she tells is about John, a sixteen-year-old boy admitted to the hospital where she worked on a Sunday afternoon. He was critically injured and it was clear he needed a neurosurgeon to save his life:

> He had been hit on the head with a cricket ball, which is slightly smaller and much harder than a tennis ball. An x-ray was ordered and it clearly showed the round piece of skull bone, completely severed, resting on the brain. Two-thirds of the bone looked clean cut, as if done with a knife, and the other third was splintered and uneven. John was suffering from increasing intercranial pressure and, as evening turned into night, his condition became critical.
>
> At the time, our only general surgeon was away for the weekend and it was doubtful if he would have done the operation anyway. We had one modestly equipped operating room and no neurosurgical instruments to speak of. We had a German nun who was a nurse anesthetist and a Canadian volunteer nurse who taught the students in the operating room. That was the limit of our resources to help John.
>
> His parents told us later John had been named after the Archbishop of Rabaul, whom they held in great esteem, and who had died a few months before.
>
> The Archbishop's niece and her husband from Germany were visiting the [Archbishop's] mission at this time. They wanted to see where the prelate had lived and carried out his missionary life. Miraculously, the husband of the niece was a neurosurgeon.
>
> Early Monday morning, John was wheeled into our humble operating theater, and there the brilliant German doctor performed the operation that saved his life. The procedure took many hours, with the capable surgeon having to adapt to primitive instruments. He spoke only German, so translation was necessary.

When John was finally wheeled back to his hospital bed, his head swaddled in white bandages, his condition was stable. The doctor, on a tight itinerary, flew back to Germany soon after. Within days, John was up and about, and two weeks later I had my picture taken with him on the hospital lawn. In the photo, he is an alert, smiling, normal teenage boy whose life had been saved propitiously—by a relative of the Archbishop for whom he had been named.

"Neither I nor John's parents ever considered the episode a coincidence. It was a case of people being exactly where they were needed at a particular time. It was God's way of working through people and sending them to us, like angels sent to guide and protect."

Reading this amazing story, it would be hard to call this a "chance" happening, considering that a boy's life was in the balance. More likely, someone "up there" was giving a helping hand.

൦ૐૐ ൦ૐૐ ൦ૐૐ ൦ૐૐ

Robert O'Shea of Reeds Spring, Missouri, has often found help in a time of need. He says he interprets these incidents as signs that "my guardian angel has been looking after me once again."

One of the experiences he relates occurred after he and his wife had been vacationing with friends in Fort Myers, Florida. They had to travel through several states to drive back to their home in Missouri. After they crossed the Georgia state line, they saw a sign that caught their eye, "Pecans for Sale." They stopped to buy some and got into a conversation with the seller. When he asked where they had to go and found out it was Missouri, he warned them not to go by way of Memphis, Tennessee, because weather conditions were bad; the main road was closed and electric power lines were down. He suggested they head for Tullula, Mississippi.

"We reached Tullula shortly after lunch and got the weather report: rain and turning colder. When we reached the next turn, Lake Village, we were met by the state police, who informed us the road was closed. The local motels were closed; only a small restaurant and a quick stop were open. People were preparing to sleep in their cars in the parking lot of the quick stop.

"We drove to the restaurant," Mr. O'Shea continued, "and were placed at the last two available seats. Sitting at the adjoining table were two young couples. When we mentioned we were from Branson, Missouri, one of the young ladies said, 'We know you. Fifteen years ago we came down to your sandwich shop on Main Street. Remember how my sister and I came down to see you and you always had a small gift for us. Our dad owned the fudge shop around the corner. Well, you are going to come to our house and stay overnight. No way are you going to sleep in the car.'"

"How blessed can one get?" Mr. O'Shea still asks.

∞ ∞ ∞ ∞

Barbara Lewis of Delaware was at a happy point in her life, savoring some great news about her work, the day she stopped into a local Acme store to pick up some items she needed. She writes, "Suddenly I was drawn to the aisle where greeting cards are found. My eyes fell on one section: 'comfort.' I picked up a card that read, 'I'd like to take the hurt away, but sometimes we must hurt for a while. Know that I am always with you.' I'm not the kind to buy nice cards and send them to people; even when I try my best, I just don't get around to it. Yet this card seemed to stay in my hand. I thought the card would be appropriate for my daughter; she had divorced recently and could use some encouraging words." As Barbara tells it:

"My world of happiness, though, was about to change forever." In those very same hours, a tragedy took place. Her only son was "a participant in an unforgettable act of violence" that had ended with his girlfriend of six years being killed.

"Fate blessed me to receive the news when both my daughters and special friends were with me. It was then that I proceeded to give the card to my daughter. She read it and said, 'Here, Mom, you bought this for yourself.'

"I know now that the message inside was sent from a Higher Source who knows my destiny. I often repeat the words from that card to get to the next moment of my life," Barbara wrote. Her son is on death row in Delaware, and she is actively working to raise consciousness nationwide to end the death penalty in the United States, which remains the only Western industrialized nation that practices execution.

ॐ ॐ ॐ ॐ

I met Sam Silverstein of Torrington, Connecticut, when I did a story on him. He is the author of a remarkable book that has taken some thirty years to get published, called *Child-Spirit*. It is about the spiritual experiences children have, of which adults are unaware. Sam had been a teacher for many years and early in his career had been assigned an art class. It was in observing the drawings of children that he made a fascinating discovery—many of the images the youngsters committed to paper came from their own visualizations of otherworldly people and places, some of these being angels and cosmic journey destinations. He told their stories in his book.

Sam, now retired and a widower, kept me spellbound with stories about his own personal experiences, all of them decidedly God-related. He also related a coincidence from his World War II days that literally saved his life, a coincidence he believes was indeed God giving him a helping hand.

The story takes place in October 1943 in the mountains of Italy, when Sam was a lieutenant in the U.S. Army infantry. They had gotten sudden attack orders which involved going over a mountain. "The jeeps, the bedrolls, and other comforts had to be left behind," said Sam, adding that he dressed as warmly as possible, knowing it could be really cold in the mountains, even in October. As the day wore on, all the men were tired and hungry. Apparently soldiers must have traveled this way before them because Sam saw parts of a K-ration that one must have thrown away. He also saw a small package and picked it up. It was a plastic "gas cape," still in its container. "The gas cape was a large, heavy plastic-bag type structure that soldiers were issued when we first arrived in Italy. It would be used in case of a gas attack from the enemy. The plastic cape would go over the body for possible protection—but most soldiers seldom carried them, or, as in this case, probably threw it away to reduce the load that one had to carry."

Sam picked up the gas cape in case he might need it. By the time the soldiers got high in the mountains, the cold had really settled in. None of them had sleeping bags. They just had to try to get some sleep on the cold ground. Sam tried to compress himself into a position where he could conserve his body heat, and he fell asleep for a while, but then he woke up from the cold. He lay there shivering, trying to think of ways to survive, when he remembered the gas cape. He opened it and crawled inside, but after a momentary warming, he started shivering again.

Then, suddenly, he heard a sound, like a whimper that an animal might make. It seemed so close. "Moving my hand out of the plastic bag, I reached out, thinking that perhaps I could touch the animal. My hand did touch an animal that was lying there by my head, next to a rock. The animal was shivering, the same way I was shivering," said Sam.

"My hand skimmed over the furry animal, and I soon recognized it to be a dog, a young dog. Thinking to myself that here I was shivering from the cold, and there the dog was shivering from the cold, why not bring him in under the gas cape and we'd shiver together— but at least we'd have each other's company. So my hand reached over and grabbed the puppy's fur by the neck and pulled him in with me, inside the plastic bag.

"And then a wonderful thing happened! As I hugged the puppy close to me—and he cuddled up close to my body—I felt the warmth of his body entering my body. He must have felt the warmth of my body, too, because suddenly we both stopped shivering."

In the morning, the puppy was still asleep in Sam's arms. Sam then moved out of his makeshift sleeping bag, stretching a little to get the kinks out of his body. "I turned to the puppy to give him a pat of 'thanks' for keeping me warm, but the young dog was nowhere to be seen. I looked about quickly to see where he might be—but he had disappeared completely. It was only about one minute of time from when the dog climbed out of the bag to when I started looking for him. The four or five soldiers nearby didn't see any puppy. I wondered what happened to him."

What could explain the presence of a puppy high in the desolate mountains north of Alife, Italy? Why did the puppy appear next to Sam's head? Why did the puppy disappear so quickly in the morning? One thing Sam knows is that this puppy probably saved him from illness or complications from severe loss of body heat, and so he's not about to relegate this remarkable help to chance.

"Now, so many years later, when I've learned the different ways God can act, I believe sending me the puppy could have been God giving me a helping hand," Sam affirms.

Chapter 5

Comforting Coincidences that Affirm, Help, and Heal

S ometimes coincidences can have a therapeutic effect, or they can be like frosting on a cake, not signifying or stimulating any major change, but bringing about a feeling of great comfort or even healing.

One of these stories came from Marie DiGiammarino, published in *The Catholic Post*. Here is Marie's story, in her words:

> About ten years ago, I was employed as a music therapist in a large residential facility for adolescents with mental retardation. One of the boys I worked with had dark hair and eyes like mine, was about my height and weight, and liked music. As a result of our similar looks and common interests, my coworkers said he could pass as my brother.
>
> My "brother" was about twelve years old and was physically strong for his age, but was barely verbal—functioning at about a three-year-old level. He often had severe temper tantrums that were dangerous to himself and others, but in his quieter moments, he liked to strum a guitar. I also enjoyed the guitar and had been wanting one of my own, but hadn't taken the time to look for one.
>
> That Friday, as Labor Day weekend was about to begin, my "brother" was sent to the campus hospital with a severe case of

bronchitis. For some reason he was on my mind all weekend. By Monday, I felt a strong need not only to visit him, but also to stop at the local department store to buy him a toy guitar.

I was hoping to spend about two or three dollars at most, but the only guitar I found cost seven dollars. I bought it anyway and went to the hospital. There I was told that the boy had been having severe temper tantrums since his arrival and had even destroyed some of the furniture in his hospital room.

When I gave him the guitar, he sat down immediately and began to strum and hum. His surprised hospital attendant commented he had not thought the boy capable of doing anything constructive. He then arranged staff visitations and leisure activities for the remainder of the hospital stay and the tantrums greatly diminished.

That night my mother, unaware of how I had spent the day, called me long distance from her home several states away. She had been to a church auction that afternoon and had bought me a present—a secondhand guitar in good condition, for exactly seven dollars!

Certainly this couldn't have been just a chance occurrence. It was an affirmation of Marie's kindness and love. The "coincidence" illustrated that good acts often have a boomerang effect—what we give to others comes back like a blessing to ourselves.

 os∞ os∞ os∞ os∞

I have had so many personal experiences that convince me we are surrounded by signs that God truly does take an interest in our day-to-day lives, often by giving us a hand.

Back in the early eighties, when I had moved to Connecticut to help start a county-wide newspaper, I was renting a house. It soon became clear to me that I was an unhappy renter. I really wanted to own my own house, one that could nicely accommodate the two adult children who were then living with me. I started to sketch out what I wanted the house to have, and the centerpiece of it was a big, square room, with a fireplace that covered a wall and glass door that led to an enclosed room leading to a patio and a large back yard. In my sketch, the room also had an extension on one side where there was a bedroom and bathroom, and on the other side, a dining room and kitchen, and, of course, a hall leading to more bedrooms and bathrooms. As for how I could ever afford a house like this, I didn't bother at all with such a practical question!

When I finally contacted a real estate agent, he seemed to have a lot of time to show me houses. Yet none of the many he showed me appealed to me. It turned out that the reason he could give me so much time is that this was the end of 1982, when the real estate market was so bad in this area, you couldn't give a house away. One day I was in his office, flipping through his book of listings as he was trying to set up yet another house for me to see. My eye caught an ad that said "house with fireplace, possible mother/daughter." It was more money than I felt I could afford, but I wanted to see it. The agent took me there.

My first reaction was that I felt like the prince who was trying to get to Sleeping Beauty. The house had been unoccupied for a couple of years and was covered over with brambles. But when the agent opened the door, I walked in with my daughter, and gasped. "Oh my God, it's my house," I said, half aloud. Truly, what I was looking at matched my sketches!

It turned out that this was a sale to settle an estate. Everybody was anxious to unload the house, which had been on the market for about three years. My agent thus managed to negotiate a price that made it possible for me to buy the house.

I have often felt that God was with me through all of this, making it possible for a single mother of a large family to be able to be in the right place at the right time so as to get a house that would serve the family well. But God did more than that. God also gave me the house I wanted so badly that I could draw it.

As I was writing this book, a friend who is also a writer, Helen Weaver, not knowing about my house experience, told me about hers, which I found to be amazingly similar. Helen's mother had died in the past year and she had decided to move from the Connecticut town where they had lived together to the Woodstock, New York, area where she has friends. Anxious to get on with "the rest of my life," as she put it, Helen was looking to buy a house. Every one she saw had obvious drawbacks. She started to pray to her mother to help her. "I said, 'Mother, I really need to move this spring. Please help me find my house. I know it's out there waiting for me.'" She then wrote in her journal a one-page description of the house she would love to find.

"That was Monday night. I was due to look at houses with Natalie Shapiro of Westwood Metes and Bounds on Wednesday. On Tuesday, Natalie and I planned our itinerary. She asked, 'What was it about that house on Zena Highwoods Road you didn't like?' I said, 'What house...I don't know the road.' Natalie realized that she hadn't shown me that house after all."

When Helen saw the house, she knew immediately it was the one for her. It almost perfectly matched the description she had written. At certain places in the house, she "felt the presence of my parents so strongly, I almost started to cry. Once back in my car, I did cry, and thanked Mother and Dad for helping me find my house."

Now, of course, it could be merely a coincidence that the day after Helen prayed to her mother for help, the real estate agent happened to remember a house for sale on Zena Highwood Road. And it could be simply a coincidence that the house matched Helen's written description of what she so truly wanted. But Helen wouldn't buy that. She knows her unexpected good luck was linked to the heavens.

಄ ಄ ಄ ಄

Another time when I personally was blessed with a comforting coincidence is most unforgettable. It happened in New York City, around ten at night. I had been at the Manhattan School of Music that evening, with all my children, enjoying the greatest experience I had ever had—attending a performance of the opera *Carmen*, listening to my daughter Mary sing the lead. After the performance, my son Paul was escorting me to Port Authority to get my bus home. We had just crossed Fortieth Street at Eighth Avenue when a big man bounded toward me, pulled my purse right out of my hand, and began to run. Paul shouted after him that he couldn't do that to his mother, and ran after him.

I was terrified. I had always been taught to let them take the purse, because you never know if they have a weapon. I was screaming at Paul to come back. At that moment, a tall, gentle-looking young man was next to me and started talking calmly to me. "The police are right across the street," he said. "Let's tell them and they'll take care of it."

We crossed the street together and the police ordered me to go back to where I had been standing and wait. The young man crossed back with me. I thanked him, expecting he'd go on his way, but he insisted on staying with me. We got talking, I introduced myself, and he said his name was Michael. He kept trying to assure me that Paul would be all right.

It was about fifteen minutes later when I saw Paul running toward me. I ran up to him, thanking God. Paul asked me if I was all right. I said, "yes, thanks to Michael, this fine young man," and turned to point to him. But he wasn't there. He was nowhere in sight.

I have often wondered, could it have been only a coincidence that a young man took the time to give comfort to a frightened woman on a street corner in Manhattan? Or was Michael there, sent by God to calm my fears? The fact that his name was Michael—like the great angel—wasn't lost on me either!

∽ ∽ ∽ ∽

A letter to me from a woman who only signed her name as Anne Marie, from New Castle, Delaware, told of a coincidence that was an instant response to a core-deep wish. Anne Marie's mother had died and it had been impossible for her husband and six children to be with her for the funeral. Her five brothers and sisters were there, but Anne Marie felt a loneliness. As she wrote, "Early in the morning after Mom died, I was looking out the kitchen window thinking how often my friend Jenny and I had met on the corner over the years, and I wished desperately that I could call her over then." But Jenny had moved far away to Texas.

Anne Marie continued, "Just then, the doorbell rang. When I opened it, there stood Jenny with a huge bowl of macaroni salad. Unknown to me, she and her son had decided to fly 'home' that week for a visit. I didn't have my husband or children to comfort me through the viewing or funeral, but God sent me the next closest person." Closest friends to this day, Anne Marie and Jenny attribute this blessed reunion to a God-incidence.

∞ ∞ ∞ ∞

In many coincidences, what is apparent is how deeply connected people who are related to each other in one way or another may be. Time and again I am told or I read about a strange occurrence that points out the strong linkage that can exist between two related people, sometimes not consciously known by one or either of them.

Television's Bill Beutel, former WABC-TV anchorman, tells a story in the January 1993 issue of *Guideposts* magazine that underscores connection, in this one, a father-daughter bond. The newscaster was awakened one early morning. The numbers on his digital clock said 5:29 A.M. He tried to get a bit more sleep, but couldn't. He was wide awake. A few hours later, he was approached by a police officer and told to call home immediately. One of his four children, Heather, had been in a bad car accident. When he got the details of the accident, he found out that the 911 call for emergency services had come "in at exactly 5:29 A.M., the very moment that I was jolted awake in New York. I could not dismiss this as coincidence."

It was three weeks before Heather came out of a coma, and it was a long, hard road back to health. She had awakened from the coma "with a hunger for God," wrote her father, who confessed that as he watched her "lean on God," he began to do the same. "It was as if at 5:29 on that fateful morning both my daughter and I began a spiritual journey together," wrote Mr. Beutel. Some might still call this coincidence, but not the anchorman. He says, "On that soft summer morning I awoke to more than a family tragedy. I was awakened to faith."

Married couples have their own coincidence stories that point out how the bond between them shows up in sometimes amazing ways. Stuart and Laura Brush of Woodbury, Connecticut, told me with big smiles, "We're a very connected couple." Stuart, a minister, bought his wife a Valentine's Day card when he was in New York City, and Laura bought a Valentine's card for her husband in a Connecticut shop. When they opened them, they found that both were the same valentine!

One of the nice things about God's surprises is that they are often just a simple touch, like a brief caress that brings a smile or a feeling of warmth.

Mary Kramer of Cincinnati, Ohio, tells of the time back in 1969 when her Aunt Clara was critically ill. She was in a nursing home, her money running out, and she wanted to go home. But there was no one who could give her the skilled care she needed. Mary was her "caregiver," and she needed some heavenly help. She had seen that the canonization of Blessed Julie Billiart, a French Sister of Notre Dame who had worked with the sick and the poor, was coming up on June 21 of that year, and so she decided to call on soon-to-be Saint Julie. She prayed to her, asking that she be given some direction on that day.

Well, the 21st came and went with no answer. And then, on the morning of the 22nd, Aunt Clara died peacefully. Mary figured she had an answer to her prayer—even if it was a day late. But then she read the day's paper and found an account of Blessed Julie's canonization—to take place on June 22!

After the funeral, she had to dismantle Aunt Clara's apartment. "In the first drawer that I opened, right on top of the contents, was this picture of St. Julie, looking up at me with that famous smile! Sometimes we need—and get—something special," Mary wrote.

ocos ocos ocos ocos

Back in 1983, I interviewed the former actress of television and movies, Susan Saint James, a lovely woman who cherishes her Catholic roots. She was nursing her baby son, who had been born on December 30, 1982, to her and her husband, Richard Ebersol—an independent television producer formerly with NBC-TV—and was named for his grandfather, Charles Ebersol of Litchfield, Connecticut. Coincidentally, she said, the baby had been born at Charlotte Hungerford Hospital in Torrington, Connecticut, practically in the same space where his father had entered the world thirty-five years earlier.

"The chances of that happening are about a zillion to one," Ms. Saint James had commented, adding another coincidental note—the nurse who assisted her in labor had been in her husband's eighth-grade class.

What made this a comforting coincidence was that here was a couple who had spent so much of their lives in the entertainment field, now having come full circle back to the values that meant the most to them—family, community, and God.

ocos ocos ocos ocos

Sometimes coincidences have a lasting effect, guiding the direction of a person's life. Others bring a benefit, comfort, learning, or maybe just a smile to others, perhaps for generations, like this tale of Marco Polo.

Born in Venice in 1254, Marco Polo was fifteen when his father and uncle, who had traveled as merchants to the kingdom of Kublai Khan in the Orient, decided to return there, this time bringing Marco along. He almost didn't make it to the Great Desert. With sand in his lungs and fever from the glaring sun, Marco Polo just wanted to lie down and die. Luckily, Kublai Khan had what we would call a "telegraph system" of beating drums, which enabled him to get the message that three travelers were on their way and one of them was near death.

When Marco Polo opened his eyes, he was in the unbelievable city of Xanadu, the capital of the Mongolian Empire. Now his adventure had begun. He developed a lasting friendship with Kublai Khan. They both shared the cultures of their countries and gained great respect for each other. Marco Polo, together with his father and uncle, remained in China twenty years.

When they got back to Venice, they were scoffed at. No one remembered them. But when they began sharing the riches they had brought back from China, and telling the tales they had learned and lived, they became the talk and the darlings of the town. Marco's nickname, in fact, became "Marco Millions!"

Three years after Marco Polo's return to Venice, Genoa declared war on Venice and the adventurer, now thirty-eight, joined in the battle. By bad luck, or fate, he was taken prisoner by the Genoese. It was a boring situation for both the prisoners and the captors, so Marco started entertaining them by telling stories of his travels in the Orient, always pointing out that China possessed a culture as ancient and beautiful as that of Greece or Rome.

One of the prisoners happened to be a writer by the name of Rusticiano. He became fascinated with the stories and thought they'd make a great travel book. He started writing them down, and his material became the famed documentary, *Travels of Marco Polo*.

If Marco Polo had not volunteered for battle, had not been taken prisoner, had not tried to contain boredom by entertaining the other men with his stories—and if a writer had not been among them—that rich recounting might have ended with the death of the adventurer. We might never have had the pleasure of reading about his fantastic travels.

ক্ষত ক্ষত ক্ষত ক্ষত

A similar coincidence accounts for why we have great detail about the life of Samuel Johnson, a man close to my heart because we both were born on September 18 and both chose journalism and writing as our professions. This eighteenth-century genius was a master of wit, conversation, and ideas. He was also a wise, good natured, honest, and tolerant man, always full of laughter, who loved people, life, and God.

It so happened that a Scotsman named James Boswell, a lawyer and a journalist, became a great admirer of Johnson. He wanted very much to meet him and had expressed this wish to a friend of his in London, an actor named Thomas Davies, who also owned a bookstore. Davies knew Johnson and would entertain Boswell by imitating his voice and manners, repeating many of the witty writer's sayings.

Then, on a Monday, May 16, 1763, Boswell was sitting in the back parlor of Davies' book shop when, unexpectedly, Johnson walked in. He was a bit gruff with the young man—Boswell was twenty-two and Johnson, fifty-three at the time—but they met again a week later, got along well, and became good friends. It was the beginning of an incredibly close relationship, with Boswell eventually becoming the biographer who would immortalize Johnson in his detailed book, *The Life of Samuel Johnson*. I tend to believe that Johnson entered the bookstore on that day and time, when Boswell was there, because the world was supposed to have the kind of biography only a dedicated person like Boswell could write.

ᔆᔆ ᔆᔆ ᔆᔆ ᔆᔆ

I have received many letters from people who have shared brief stories with me, stories that gave them comfort, or moments to remember about what they felt was God's goodness.

Don and Rita McCarthy of Westport, Massachusetts, are among those who have written to me. They told me they have noted many unusual experiences that they can only call God-incidences. One happened when they were touring Ireland and visited the Franciscan monastery in Killarney. "We also toured the cemetery and really got a shock. One tombstone read James A. McCarthy and Nora T. McCarthy, the same names as my parents buried at Riverside cemetery in Fairhaven!" said Don.

The couple also told me about a cherry tree they have in their backyard—one they never planted. "It appeared as a twig on a rock the day after my mother was buried. The twig has since grown into a beautiful tree," wrote Don. "The symmetry of the tree is interesting. It has a split base (mother and father) and three main branches off the base (brother, sister, and myself)." It branches out again, he says, into one, two and three shoots, equal to the number of children each of them has. "Interesting!" Don comments.

ομο ομο ομο ομο

Father Frank Burger, a retired priest of Grand Junction, Missouri, sent me his story, an incident that happened while he was a chaplain at Leila Hospital in Battle Creek. "I took communion around each day after Mass to all the Catholic patients. One day the Sister there told me a new patient had come in and asked me to make sure to include her on my list. About 2 P.M., it came to me that I had forgotten to include her, and so I went at once to bring her communion.

"I had just gotten into the room when the phone rang. She picked it up. It was her son, a priest in Chicago. He told her he wanted to talk to a priest about how things were for her in the hospital. She put me on the phone. I believe the Lord permitted me to forget her in the morning so that I would be there when her son called, to reassure him about his mother."

All one could say with certainty is that a coincidence occurred, but no one could refute that this synchronous "meeting" was certainly a comforting moment for both the ill woman and her devoted priest-son.

ομο ομο ομο ομο

I call this next one the "Gregory miracle," sent to me by Mary Caputo of Dover, Delaware. Her story dates back to 1954, when she had given birth to a second son, her fourth child. Her mother had come from New Jersey to stay with the family while Mary was in the hospital. As it got to be the day before she was to go home, they had a problem. They needed to have a name for the baby and no one could agree on one.

That day her mother got a call to return to New Jersey because Mary's brother Dominick was seriously ill and not expected to live. She left not knowing what the baby's name would be, asking only that they choose a good saint's name. Before the day was over, Mary, her children, and husband had picked a name—Gregory.

"The following day I called my mom to find out about my brother and she related the following: Upon entering the hospital room, she saw my brother was very ill and in an oxygen tent. When he saw my mother, he said, 'Mom, I'm so happy to see you. I sure thought I was a goner, but I saw St. Gregory and he brought me back.' Needless to say, when I told my mother we had named the baby Gregory, she was so very happy. My brother remained in the hospital for three months. He was able to see the baby from the window of his hospital bed. He died later, in August 1954.

"I know there is some significance to this incident," Mary affirmed, still touched by what happened more than forty years ago.

છે છે છે છે

Donald Niebauer of Pennsylvania sent me another story of a "coincidence" that brought him great comfort. In September of 1993, his mother was dying. A eucharistic minister brought a host to their home, but his mother could not swallow it. Donald, a trained minister to the sick when he worked in Florida in the eighties, broke off a tiny piece of the host and, dissolving it in water, helped her to be nourished with the Body of Christ in the eucharist. He consumed the rest of the host. She died a few days later.

On Mother's Day in 1994, he writes, "I went to communion at my church in Fairview. When I looked at the host that I received from the eucharistic minister, it had a small piece removed from it, just like the one I removed for my mother that day a few months earlier. I consumed this host on Mother's Day, just as I consumed the remainder of my mother's host that day before she died."

Chapter 6

Coincidences that Lead a Person from Despair to a New Life

Rev. Stuart Brush and his wife Laura have been my friends for many years. We met when I interviewed them for the work they were doing with a support group called Survivors of Homicide. Their son Dean had been murdered when he worked for a pizza store and was making a delivery. His life was taken away by street youth for the few dollars he had collected. I was particularly impressed by this clergyman for his wisdom, gentleness, and what I could sense was his outreach to others. That feeling was confirmed when I confided that, like them, I was a parent who had also lost a son to a cruel murderer. Their empathy was healing. I told them I was privileged to meet people so Christlike.

Imagine my surprise when Stuart told me he had not always been in this place of peace. In fact, he had almost lost his very being several decades earlier when he had become an around-the-clock drinker. It was a remarkable coincidence that dramatically brought him out of the darkness he had fallen into and put him on the path to a new life.

As Stuart told me, he would not acknowledge that he was an alcoholic. He would only say he had a "problem" with his drinking, and that he could fix it himself, by exercising willpower. "I had always achieved success through personal struggle. For me life was a chessboard on which I could move my pieces with mastery and cunning." His denial went on until he started going for the bottle at seven in the morning and kept at it all day long. Then, finally, he was forced by his wife and friends in his parish to face the truth and go to an alcoholism rehab center.

At the rehab center, he was being told to acknowledge that willpower wouldn't work. He needed to turn to a Higher Power. While he would appear to agree, in his head he was still saying arrogantly, "I can master it."

He had gone to the rehab center in early December and he vividly remembers being at one of the sessions, sitting there with his arms folded, symbolically removing himself from the others. He was somewhat jolted when the unit director suddenly said to all of them, "That fellow over there with his arms folded is the one person in this room I doubt will ever get better."

For days after that he kept hearing those words over and over in his head, and yet he didn't believe the director was right. As Christmas approached, Stuart knew he couldn't go home, but he asked for and got permission to attend Christmas Eve services at a nearby church. When he got there, everybody was given a candle by the usher upon entering. Stuart took a candle and found a seat. He recalls sitting there, filled with "shame, guilt, and remorse" as he looked around and saw the happy families celebrating Christmas together, while he was separated from his family.

"After the music and the message, the lights dimmed and the candlelighting ceremony began. As the usher approached, I lifted my candle, but, horror of horrors, the light went zap and was gone! Of all the hundreds of candles in the sanctuary, mine was the one that wouldn't light," said Stuart. "I sat there in my darkness."

He was unprepared for his reaction, the overwhelming sense that it was not by chance that he was left without the light of the candle. He felt overwhelmed and hopeless. Back in his room, he slumped on the bed and thought about his life. "The unlighted candle seemed to signify its futility in spite of all my striving and willpower," he told me.

His eyes fell upon a little ceramic crèche that his wife Laura had given him, with an angel looking over Jesus, and in that moment, he said, "I got a message. Christ was born in the darkness, in a cave—in a place like the bowels of this place where I was, in rehab. I knew then that Christ was born for people like me, for people in the darkness."

Stuart started to weep and he felt himself surrender to a truth he had been resisting—that Christ, not himself, was in charge.

"Instead of a lighted candle, my Higher Power came to me that night in a place where he can be born most powerfully: a broken, contrite heart," Stuart said. This was the end of his drinking and the beginning of his new life.

To this day, Stuart and Laura remember the candle that wouldn't light, and they believe that it was a gift from the Lord, who loved Stuart enough to make him see that he was stuck in a dark place where a false pride held him captive. The candle in his hand was, as he was, incapable of giving light. It was a powerful message Stuart received on that Christmas Eve, triggered by the "coincidence" of a candle that resisted the firelight.

ൟ ൟ ൟ ൟ

The late Jeanne Mitchell Biancolli was another dear friend who also found her way out of darkness because of an apparent coincidence.

Jeanne was an extraordinary violinist. She made her debut in New York in 1947, and the first reviews called her "a bright young star in the violin galaxy." After that she played on the major concert stages worldwide. But her life didn't turn out to be just roses on a stage. She gave up performing when she married Louis Biancolli, music critic for the long gone *World Telegram and Sun*. She became the mother of two daughters, and after a few years, when her husband became unexpectedly ill, she turned to teaching to support her family.

In the early seventies, Jeanne faced another crisis, her own serious illness from kidney failure and heart trouble. She didn't belong to any religious denomination, yet, as she went into the operating room, she began for the first time calling on God, asking to survive. Amazingly, she did come through this crisis, but then life went on as usual. God was not very much in the picture as she picked up the heavy responsibilities of her life.

And then one day Jeanne was driving back to her home in Connecticut from a New York appointment, when she became distracted and found herself in tears. She kept hearing a voice inside her head telling her, "You haven't been good to God." These thoughts affected her so strongly that she didn't realize she had missed her turn and was now driving aimlessly on an unfamiliar road. She didn't even know what town she was in.

Then she saw a sign that caught her attention. It said "Abbey of Regina Laudis." As she told me many times, Jeanne thought this was a monastery for Anglican monks. She drove up to the door and rang the bell. She was warmly welcomed by a nun, who had great compassion for this woman who was crying as if her heart were broken. Jeanne later discovered that this was a monastery of Benedictine nuns.

In Jeanne's words, the sisters there "took me from nowhere to what I consider the end of the line—God." At this Abbey, this wonderful woman and astounding violinist found her "home," as she once told me. She was baptized into the Catholic church in March 1983, and she continued going to this Abbey until her death in 1995.

We spoke many times about the "coincidence" of her losing her way that day in the car and stumbling upon the Abbey, which helped her find her life again. And we would laugh and say, "Of course, it was not a coincidence." It was God's way of guiding Jeanne to a place of hope, where she could find the peace she needed to go on with her difficult life.

Jeanne's greatest talent was her virtuoso playing of solo violin. She played at the memorial service for my son John, also a violinist, after his death. John and his wife Nancy were murdered in their newly purchased home in Montana on August 12, 1993, blown away by a 9 mm semiautomatic gun in the hands of the eighteen-year-old son of the couple from whom my children had purchased their home. The highlight of the memorial service for John was Jeanne's solo violin rendition of a Bach requiem.

There is a postscript to this story of my friendship with Jeanne. On the morning after I got the news of Jeanne's death from a brain hemorrhage, I was awakened by the beautiful sounds of a solo violin filling my bedroom. I jumped up, literally expecting to see Jeanne! It took a few moments before I realized that the music was coming from my bedside radio. To this day, I don't know how my radio happened to be on. I had not turned it on, nor had I set the radio alarm. Also, wasn't it strange that when the radio went on what happened to be playing was solo violin?

Never before nor since have I heard a solo violin rendition on that radio station. I truly believe that another force was at work in my bedroom that morning, allowing Jeanne to come to me to say a last goodbye. It was the greatest gift that could be given to a friend.

ॐ ॐ ॐ ॐ

Even on the pages of history one can find stories of great people who faced moments of despair, when life seemed doomed to darkness. One of these men was Sam Houston, the great statesman who was the leader in the struggle to win Texas for the United States. But for an unusual occurrence, he might never have survived long enough to get to Texas.

Sam Houston was certainly a remarkable man, coming from what could be called a long line of fighting Irish, who came to America to find freedom. When he was fourteen, his father died and his widowed mother moved with her nine sons from Virginia to Tennessee. After a year, his brothers apprenticed him to the village storekeeper, but Sam, already six feet tall and strong-willed, rebelled. He ran away and joined a tribe of Cherokees, taking the name Black Raven. He stayed with them for three years.

Books have been written about his colorful life from then on—how he opened a school, and then joined the Army, fighting the Indians under General Andrew Jackson who was known as "Old

Hickory"; how he was so badly wounded he was given up for dead, yet survived because of his great resilient spirit; how he later studied law, was elected to Congress and then elected Governor of Tennessee. While Governor, he married the beautiful Eliza Allen, but the marriage was brief. His wife left him for another man, one she had long loved, and Sam was left to live with the scandal and disgrace.

It was more than he could bear, and so he resigned from the governorship and took a boat headed toward the wilderness, not knowing or caring about the future of his life. He was, in fact, so depressed that he contemplated suicide by throwing himself overboard and ending his life in the waters. Then, at that very moment "a giant eagle swooped close to the deck, then flew screaming into the sunset. Sam's spirits rose; he felt that the bird's flight indicated a future for him in the West."

Again he sought a haven with the Cherokees and for a while he drank heavily. But when unprincipled white men began ravishing the land of the Cherokees, Sam went to Washington to see his old friend Andrew Jackson, now President, to get justice for the Cherokees. Phase two of this determination to help his Indian friends was to travel to Texas, which at that time was part of Mexico. He never expected the destiny that awaited him there—how he would become chief of the Texas forces, design the battle of the Alamo, and lead his men to rout the enemy, saving Texas forever from Mexican domination.

A few years later, as president of Texas, Sam Houston was instrumental in getting Texas annexed to the United States. The great sadness for him, an abolitionist, was that he could not persuade Texas to stay with the Union when the Civil War began. When he refused to swear allegiance to the Confederacy, he was deposed from his position as Governor of Texas in 1861. He died two years later.

Today, the name of Sam Houston is evermore respected and identified with his beloved Texas. Yet, but for an eagle swooping down on him as he stood in despair and disgrace, weighing the choice between going on or ending his life, he might never have gone to Texas. How different our history might be if Sam Houston had not lived. What was that eagle—just a bird, or a messenger from a higher source?

ogo ogo ogo ogo

One of the most mysterious coincidences I encountered in reading so many biographies of famous people over the years was what happened to the English poet Francis Thompson, best known for his remarkable poem, "The Hound of Heaven."

Francis, born in 1859 to Charles and Mary Thompson, both converts to the Catholic faith, was troubled from an early age. After rejecting an early attraction to the priesthood, he decided to follow in his father's track and become a doctor. But, during medical school he became very ill and had to drop out. Unfortunately, that illness introduced him to opium, a devastating addiction that, along with alcoholism, plagued him all his life. By the time he was twenty-six, he had alienated his father—who did all he could yet failed to help his son heal—and moved to London, trying to pick up odd jobs, yet falling more and more into squalor, even becoming homeless at times.

Miserable, starving, and in rags, Francis was wandering the streets of London when he was stopped by a stranger, Mr. McMaster, a churchman who made a habit of trying to save the souls of vagrants. When Francis told him, in effect, to get lost, McMaster answered, "If you won't let me save your soul, let me save your body." It was a turning point, though temporary. Being given food and lodging, along with books and paper and pen, Francis began to write the prose and poetry that filled his head, sending some of these to magazines, but having them all rejected.

Before long, he was back on the alcohol and opium, and McMaster had to turn him away. Francis had reentered the underworld. Only one thing had given him a little hope. He believed there was one place his work could be published, and that was *Merry England,* the magazine put out by two notable English people of letters, Wilfred and Alice Meynell, both Catholics, who might understand him. He sent a manuscript he had written at McMaster's home, titled "Paganism," to them with a cover letter and began to hope. When he heard nothing after six months, his hope degenerated to despair. In a memoir of her father and Francis Thompson, Viola Meynell, daughter of Wilfred and Alice, tells what happened to the then unpublished poet, who was at that time sleeping at night under the arches of Covent Garden:

"It was in an empty space of ground behind the market where the gardeners throw their rubbish that he had resolved on suicide. He spent all his remaining pence on laudanum [opium], one large dose, and he went there one night to take it. He had swallowed half, when he felt an arm laid on his wrist, and looking up he saw Chatterton standing over him and forbidding him to drink the other half. I asked him when he told me of it how he had known it was Chatterton. He said, 'I recognized him from the pictures of him—besides, I knew that it was he before I saw him.'"

Now, who was Chatterton? Thomas Chatterton was an English poet who lived from 1752 to 1770. He was a teenager when he wrote his poems, under the pen name of "Rowley." Like Thompson, he left home to go to London, living in a destitute situation, often on bread and water. In despair and disillusioned about his perceived failure at everything, Chatterton committed suicide by taking poison, three months before his eighteenth birthday.

By not killing himself, Thompson lived another twenty years, literally "adopted" by the Meynells. The manuscript sent to *Merry England* had somehow gotten misplaced under piles of other papers and it was six months before Wilfrid and his wife noticed it. An essay and one of the poems were worthy of publication. They published them, and thus began a relationship that became deeply cemented in love and lasted for life, until Francis died—from the abuses of his body from drugs, poor nutrition, and, I believe, psychological traumas—on November 13, 1907 at the age of forty-eight. Thanks to the Meynells, a poet was allowed to be born, and the world given the gift of his genius.

But it astounds me to think of how Francis Thompson's light would have been extinguished on that lonely, garbage-strewn road in London if a remarkable coincidence hadn't occurred. *Someone* pulled him out of the act of killing himself. Could it have been Chatterton, returning to earth by some miraculous occurrence to save another man like himself who was destined to give poetry to the world? I find it really amazing that Thompson said he saw Chatterton, who had committed suicide, while he himself was in the act of killing himself.

Was the powerful hand he felt not only saving him from self-inflicted death, but also giving him the message of how wrong it is to kill oneself?

We'll never really know exactly what happened, but perhaps it is enough to know that Thompson was saved because, at the moment of his planned death, the hand of a man pulled him back to life.

ༀ ༀ ༀ ༀ

In 1994, the KATV Publishing House, Inc. in Hoboken, New Jersey, sent me a book to review called *The Muselmann, The Diary of a Jewish Slave Laborer,* by David Matzner, with David Margolis. The author, a rabbi, had survived five years in twenty slave labor camps during the infamous period of the Nazi Holocaust. In 1950, Rabbi Matzner came to America with his wife Lucia, also a Holocaust survivor, settling in Florida and devoting much of his life to helping the needy. Before his death on August 15, 1986, he wrote his memoir.

I remember the touching story he told of trainloads of Jews arriving at Auschwitz, himself among them. They all had to go through a checking point, where SS men were deciding where each prisoner would go—to the gas chamber or work. As he related:

> Suddenly, looking around to the brightly shining lights, I saw my brother Abraham; his back was to me, but I recognized the way he moved his shoulders. Yes, I was sure it was him, my brother, moving forward in the same line as I, lifting his head. There were twenty or twenty-five men between us. I began to shout his name, but he couldn't hear me. Without thinking of the guards, I stepped out of line and ran to be with him, to ask how and when he had been taken, where his wife and children were. I reached him and grasped his shoulders. He turned around—it was a stranger.
>
> Some SS men several feet behind me, stepped into the line. Together with the few men behind me, I passed the hand-waving SS man and went to the right. Behind me the entire line had been cut off and sent to the gas chamber. The image of my

brother, the illusion of having seen him, saved me.... During the years of my imprisonment in concentration camps and forced-labor camps, and even to this day, I have never found a plausible explanation for what happened to me that night in Auschwitz. Was it all coincidence, or was it part of some law of life far beyond human comprehension? Had my parents' blessings materialized in some supernatural form? To this day I am inclined to believe the latter, as I am strongly convinced of the living power of the soul. Some say a miracle is an event that contradicts known scientific laws. But does science know all the laws of nature, all that is in heaven and earth? The sight of my brother was an illusion, the effects of which saved my life. For me, it was a miracle.

In that moment when despair gave way to a prayer of thanksgiving for being saved, I believe that Rabbi Matzner was put on a path of trust that he would prevail. In his own words, he revealed, "Physically, biologically, I existed in that place. But mentally, I remained aloof, registering what happened to me with ear and eye, but keeping it from penetrating the inner core of my being.... Each morning I would say aloud to myself and to those near me, 'Today is one more day. This day, too, we shall overcome with the help of God.' Then I would recite a few lines of that beautiful prayer, *Adon Olom* ('Lord of the World'), which ends with the sentence, 'The Almighty is with me, I shall not fear.'"

This remarkable man wrote his memoir to be "a testimony that no suffering can ever suppress the will of human beings to live." He had help in getting to that conviction—the image of his brother in a time of fatal danger. I believe, with Rabbi Matzner, that it would be trivial and false to call this incident at Auschwitz "just a coincidence." He himself expressed it best—"a law of life far beyond human comprehension."

Chapter 7

When Coincidence Pays Off in a Practical Way

Most of the time we hesitate to ask God for practical help, especially money. We have the idea that it's a bit obscene to muddy the spiritual waters by mentioning physical needs. We'd rather believe that God knows what we need and will provide it for us. Well, more and more I've come to believe that both are true—that God answers our prayers for practical help and often gives us a surprise bonus—especially as I hear "coincidence" stories about practical gifts, including money, given to someone at times when this help was sorely needed.

The most remarkable documented instances about receiving badly needed money in a physically unexplainable way were reported by people who gave testimonies for the canonization of St. Thérèse of Lisieux. One of these stories came from Mother Mary Carmela, prioress of the Discalced Carmelite convent in the town of Gallipoli, Italy. The nuns there had been suffering for several years from extreme poverty. It so happened that the prioress had gotten a copy of the autobiography of Sister Thérèse and had read this to the community. She decided to make a special appeal to the Lord for three days to help them find money, through the intercession of the Little Flower.

At the end of the Triduum, Mother Carmela had a dream in which she felt a hand touch her and a sweet voice tell her that she would receive five hundred francs to pay the debt of her community. Suddenly she felt herself outside her cell, in the company of a young Carmelite nun so full of light that it brightened the room, who led her downstairs to the parlor and told her to open a wooden box there. She did, and the nun of the apparition deposited the five hundred francs there.

In the morning, two of the sacristans saw Mother Carmela at Mass and were troubled that she appeared in a weakened condition. She told them about her dream, and they urged her to go down to the parlor and examine the box. When she opened it, they all saw placed there the sum of five hundred francs!

Could the dream have been merely a subconscious reminder for the prioress that the money was there all along and she had forgotten about it? I believe that it was, indeed, young Sister Thérèse of Lisieux who helped out. After all, she had left a promise that she would spend her heaven "doing good on earth," and certainly helping a destitute person or place with survival funds qualifies as a heavenly gift.

∞ ∞ ∞ ∞

In September 1996, a series of coincidences occurred that resulted in financial aid for my daughter Margaret at a time when she felt somewhat desperate about yet another big bill looming over her. Years ago, Margaret, who is divorced and has two sons, bought one of those "handyman special" houses and has had to keep pouring money into it to hold it together. Her most recent problem had been a leaking roof. She had run out of pans to catch the rain pouring in! And she was concerned, knowing there was no way she would find the money to put on the new roof she needed.

Determined to keep cheerful, Margaret arranged to have a birthday dinner for me, with the family in attendance. What had helped her mood was a call from my son Paul. He told her that when he and his wife Sue arrived, they had a surprise for her—a check for some coins she had given him to appraise and sell. She told us that from Paul's tone of voice it sounded to her like the coins may have been worth a couple of hundred dollars, and she laughed, thinking this would be quite remarkable. Paul, you may recall, is a coins and medals dealer in New York City.

How she got the coins—a number of nickels and dimes with a face value of about one dollar—was "by coincidence." Several years ago she went to an estate sale and saw a box of old stationery about to be thrown out. Since she is an artist and fashion designer, beauty catches her eye, and the design on the paper was lovely. They sold her the box for fifty cents. She put the box in a closet and forgot about it for six or seven years, until this summer. Then by chance, she came upon the box, took it down, flipped through the paper, and discovered an envelope that had these coins in it. She brought them to Paul in New York.

Paul had immediately noticed that one of the coins was valuable. To get a verifying appraisal, he sent the coin to the Numismatic Guaranty Corporation of America, which authenticated it and graded it as "Extremely Fine." Paul knew then that the nickel his sister had found would be reported as the most valuable "circulation find" ever—a 1916 Indian Head, Double Die five-cent coin.

We didn't know any of this until Paul and Sue arrived for the party. And then Paul wrote a check for his sister. He had had an auction at the summer New York Coin Exposition, and Margaret's nickel went for eleven thousand dollars!

There was a lot of cheering and singing and "wow"-ing. I got the camera out. Sue was videotaping the event. We were all ecstatic. Now Margaret could get her new roof, finish the bathroom partly built for the boys, and maybe even relax a bit for the winter.

But for me, it was much more than all that. I was, as C.S. Lewis would put it, "surprised by joy." I kept looking at Paul's face and he was beaming for the gift he had been able to give his sister. I watched Margaret and heard her say how lucky she was to have a brother like Paul, who wouldn't have deceived or cheated her. I thought of how often I had prayed to the Lord my single mother's prayer—"Please Lord, let my children be a solid family; help them to always love one another." Now I was thanking God for that answered prayer.

Then we started counting the coincidences—that Margaret had come across the box that was about to be tossed in the garbage; that she had put the box away and forgotten about it; that she had rediscovered it and found the coins just at a time when she was desperate for money; that the coin appraiser was her brother, known for his honesty; and, remarkably, that the coin was worth what was for her a small fortune. We all said a resounding thanks-be-to-God, convinced that God truly gives us a hand when we most need it.

ॐ ॐ ॐ ॐ

My niece, Rose, a health professional, also had a coincidence story for me that involved money. One of her patients is a woman named Mary, a mother of three, who had been suffering a great deal from a physical infirmity. Then, suddenly, her husband died, leaving her with no money and three children to finish raising. When things got close to desperate, Mary decided it would be best to move back to her hometown in another state where she could have the help of family. The problem was money. Train transportation would be $930, a sum she simply didn't have.

She was in Rose's office, trying to be optimistic, when she saw flyers asking for people to contribute to a clothing drive at the agency where my niece works. She told Rose that she didn't have much she could give, except for an overcoat that was her husband's, still hanging in the closet. The next day Rose went to her house to pick up the coat.

She doesn't know why, but Rose told me something nudged her to check the pockets. They were empty, but then she felt something in the lining. She brought the coat to Mary and they opened the lining. There, inside, was a wad of money. When they added it up, the total came to exactly $930!

As Rose put it, Mary, who has so little, was trying to give what she could to help someone else. It is not surprising to her that the good Lord rewarded this woman with the exact amount she needed to get her life together in a better setting. I was reminded of a line by a suffering soul I had read once, "No tear of mine but Thou dost hoard and record it." And, sometimes the Lord finds a practical way to dry those tears.

಄ ಄ ಄ ಄

It's hard to characterize Bernard Baruch (1870-1965), except to call him an American original: a Greek scholar, Wall Street financier, adviser to five presidents, a public servant, an adviser to and advocate for America's farmers, a man who worked after World War II to study how atomic energy might be used creatively for peace, not destruction. Certainly, what made it possible for him to devote so much of his life to public service was the fact that he was enormously wealthy, a fortune made mostly in the stock market beginning when he was less than twenty years old.

His first stroke of luck in accumulating huge money happened by what could be called a coincidence. It was close to the turn of the century and young Bernard had invested heavily in Almagamated Copper. However, in further studying the company, he had concluded the price was too high and he began to sell. Sure enough the stock started to slump. It was one of those days that he was watching like a hawk to see how low the price would go, when the phone rang. It was his mother, reminding him that Yom Kippur was coming and she expected him to spend the Jewish holiday with his family.

At that, with no explanations to his associates, he packed up and headed to the family home. When the Exchange next opened, the stock continued to fall. Baruch's assistants tried to reach him to tell him to sell, but no luck. Then, just after noon on that day, Amalgamated Copper declared a dividend and the price started to soar. When Bernard Baruch got back to his office, he found he was now richer, by nearly a million dollars.

Given his genius, Bernard Baruch would probably have made a fortune even if he had been in the office and sold Amalgamated Copper that day. But this million got him going and he got richer, even as he kept realizing he was not a Wall Street man at heart. When he met Woodrow Wilson, the Democratic presidential candidate in 1912, this changed the entire course of Baruch's life. From then on, his money and his heart went to serve his country and humanity. He refused praise for his public service, saying, "When God and the community have been good to a man, isn't it natural that he should try to make some payment?"

Was it only a coincidence that Baruch's mother called on a day he was preoccupied with money? And was it because of his instant decision to go home and pray with his family that the Lord poured blessings on him? We don't know the answer to that. But what we do know is that America gained in uncountable ways because Bernard Baruch knew how to make and use money for the good of his country.

○ॐ○ ○ॐ○ ○ॐ○ ○ॐ○

Someone was clearly watching out for Mrs. Gerry Moore of Ohio the day she felt near despair:

> When my sons were eleven and twelve, I was their sole support. One evening I came home from work with fifty cents in my purse and enough gas in the car to get to work the next day, pay day. I had very little food in the house and I sat, defeated, saying, "Oh God, what am I going to do?" as I had to make an evening meal for my boys and lunches for the next day.
>
> At that, I found myself back in the car, driving to the nearest supermarket. When I got to the parking lot, I got out of the car, looked down, and there, lying on the ground at my feet, was a ten dollar bill, enough for the food I needed.

Can you tell me why I went to the store as I had no intention of going? It was God's way, I'm convinced, of telling me that my boys and I would be cared for.

Who could question that?

○ॐ○ ○ॐ○ ○ॐ○ ○ॐ○

This following account is another of the stories published by editor Thomas Dermody in *The Catholic Post*. It was sent in by Father C.B. Motsett, who gave a somewhat different account of how the Lord answered a prayer having to do with money. He relates:

A number of years ago, Father Raymond Sprague and I were in White Pines State Park. As we were walking up the path to the lodge for our supper, Father Sprague looked down and picked up three twenty dollar bills.

We asked in the lodge if anybody had reported the loss. "So far, nobody," we were told. We informed them that we had found some money and gave the number of our cabin should anybody claim it.

That night when we were retiring, I said to Ray, "Let's say a prayer for the one who lost it that we will find him or her." I added, "If you or I lost that amount, we would have to go home."

The next morning I was up first and was reading the paper on a bench in front of our cabin. Suddenly, I looked up and saw two ladies coming down the main walk. One of them seemed to be worried so I said, "Pardon me, ladies, did either of you lose anything?"

The first one said "No," the other said, "Yes, I lost sixty dollars."

The first lady seemed startled. "You didn't tell me," she said.

"I didn't want to worry you," said the second woman.

I went in to get the sixty dollars. Mind you, there were at least fifty to sixty people in that park.

Some might say it was only by chance that these two women happened to be walking by the bench where the priest was sitting, and that he happened to notice one looked worried. But that's not how Father Motsett saw it. He concluded directly, "God answered our prayers."

০৯০ ০৯০ ০৯০ ০৯০

In another of the "God-incidence" stories published in *The Catholic Post*, Marietherese Creighton told about an experience her oldest son had had ten years earlier when he was a college sophomore. He had been "invited to go with a group sponsored by Divine Word Missionaries to a small Mexican village up in the mountains to work among the poor. His expenses were paid, but he needed $256.34 for his plane ticket. He was feeling sad that he probably would not be able to go." He was expecting an income tax return from working at McDonald's, but figured his return would be much smaller than the price of the plane ticket.

"What a surprise we had when he opened it and the total was exactly $256.17, only seventeen cents short of his plane ticket!" wrote his mother.

∽ ∽ ∽ ∽

A single mother who had raised three children alone wrote to me from Hawaii to tell me of a coincidence that has remained memorable for her. "How awfully poor we were so often," writes Barbara Johnson. "I remember thinking once something to the effect that, oh, if I just had fifteen dollars, I'm sure that would see me through. In the mail that very day was a plain white envelope with fifteen dollars inside. To this day, I do not know who sent it to me."

Barbara believes this mysterious gift was a result of "God's providence." "God loves us...with an infinite tenderness. And doesn't love shine brightest in little things?" Barbara asks.

∽ ∽ ∽ ∽

My friend Chuck Vrtacek sent me an account of a time when a coincidence had a practical payoff, though not in money. A fine writer who worked with me for ten years, Chuck had sadly decided he would never be able to make a real living at writing, and so he applied and was accepted for nursing school. This was a major change for him and not surprisingly he began to undergo a lot of stress. He writes:

The other night I went to see my acupuncturist for a check-up because I've been so stressed out during my first semester of school. She said my liver and heart functions were down. Nothing to be alarmed about, but for my liver, I should give up the standard things, fats, sugar, and alcohol. Just since the fall I'd developed a habit of having a single glass of wine with dinner. Anyway, later that night, after coming home from the acupuncturist, it was near bedtime so I prayed, as I always do before I go to bed. In my prayer I asked for guidance for my health.

In my mind's eye, I saw the number one hundred and seven and something told me to get my Bible and open it to page one hundred and seven. I got the Bible, placed my thumbs on the edges of the pages as one does to open a book, and it literally popped open to page one hundred and seven. The very first thing was a verse about Moses warning the Israelites about drinking too much wine. The rest of the page was a very difficult passage about how to atone for sins by bringing specific offerings to the priest, which I don't think applied to me. But talk about prayers getting answered! I guess if I damage my liver by drinking wine, I can't say I wasn't warned.

ৎ৹ ৎ৹ ৎ৹ ৎ৹

Alice Brillo of Somerset, Massachusetts wrote me a few years ago about one of her "God-incidents" that had a very practical benefit. She and her husband had been going to Florida in the winter months for health reasons and planned that year to go there to stay with a cousin who lived in a trailer park for seniors. It seems that everyone there got around on a three-wheel bike, and Alice thought this would be great for her husband, who had had several heart attacks. She knew a friend had one of these bikes and she called her to see if she wanted to sell it. To her surprise and gratitude, the friend offered to give it to her.

The problem then was how to get the bike to Florida and still stay within their budget. Alice phoned a moving company called Clithero. Again, to her surprise, she got a warm response. The owner said he would take it for no charge. He was going to Florida and all she would have to do was pick it up at the motel where he would be arriving. When he gave her the address, it turned out to be no more than ten minutes from her cousin's home. "God sure can take care of things," she wrote.

The bike turned out to be an immense gift for her husband, and when it came time to go back to Massachusetts in March, he wanted to bring the bike back too. At this very time, a neighbor told them that a mover was taking another neighbor's car back to Massachusetts and he suggested that Alice talk with the movers. She did, and couldn't believe they turned out to be the same movers who had brought the bike down. Again, Mr. Clithero transported the bike at no cost.

"Would you call this coincidence?" Alice asked. "No way. It's God-incidence. All things work out for the good to those who believe," she affirmed.

ॐ ॐ ॐ ॐ

A coincidence occurred in the life of St. Gregory the Great, circa 586, that had a very practical outcome for him. According to the story, Gregory, who had converted his home in Rome into St. Andrew's monastery and become a monk, had seen blonde, handsome Saxon slaves up for sale in the marketplace. He asked where they were from and was told Britain. He also asked if the people of that island were Christians and found out that they were pagans.

The story continues that Gregory then asked Pope Pelagius II for permission to lead some missionaries to England. When the Pope said yes, Gregory started out. But at the beginning of the trip, during a rest time when he was reading Scripture, a locust fell on the page before him. He said aloud, "Locusta," and added, that the word means "loca sta," or, in other words, "stay put." He took this as a sign that he should not go to England and abandoned his plans. That was fortunate for the church, because Pelagius died soon after when a plague struck Rome, and Gregory was elected Pope, consecrated on September 3, 590.

He never forgot his desire to Christianize Britain, however, and so in 596, he sent a mission of monks from St. Andrew's, under Augustine, prior of St. Andrew's, to that land. They were turned back, though, when they got as far as Gaul and heard stories of Saxon savagery, being informed that these blonde, handsome people "were wild beasts who preferred killing to eating, thirsted for human blood, and liked Christian blood best of all." Gregory encouraged them to go back and try again. The happy ending to this story is that they did go back and, in a few years, had accomplished their mission of converting England to Christianity.

Still, one would have to wonder whether Gregory would have made it alive if he had gone to England many years earlier when he first asked the pope for permission. Clearly God had much work for this great man to do in his lifetime of sixty-four years. Perhaps the locust landing on Gregory's open book was much more than a coincidence. It may have been a lifesaver, a practical gift from the Lord.

೦ஃ೦ ೦ஃ೦ ೦ஃ೦ ೦ஃ೦

Sometimes events with a practical outcome have a miraculous cast to them, like the situation in Poland in 1498. In that year, Poland was in danger of being overtaken by the Tartars and the Turks. History books say that some seventy thousand men of these enemy tribes were encamped between the Pruth and the Dniester rivers, getting ready to attack. The people sought out their holy preacher Ladislaus of Gielniov. He exhorted the frightened people to pray. Only their trust in God could help them in this crisis. And pray they did.

Biographers of the holy man, now Blessed Ladislaus, write that before the enemies could get their act together, the waters of both rivers began to rise, until they flooded over, covering the area. Almost immediately, the flooding was followed by freezing temperatures and a blizzard of snow. Enemy soldiers in great numbers either drowned or froze to death. The few who survived were defeated by the Polish Prince Stephen.

What was it that caused the weather to change so severely, powerfully enough to rout the enemy? The people credited the prayers of Blessed Ladislaus for their deliverance.

∞ ∞ ∞ ∞

Friends of mine, John and Maureen McNamara, of Mahopac, New York, told me of a predicament some people, including a friend of theirs, were in when they were hiking the Appalachian Trail. A severe storm had come up and their friend Ed was trying to make it to a main road. Along the way he came upon two men and a young girl, the daughter of one of them. They decided to stay together with the hope that a car would come along. Thinking practically, they agreed that if they could hitch a ride into town, they'd go, but if no car stopped, they would head back to their campsite and take their chances on sitting out the storm.

The first vehicle to come along was a pickup truck, and it went past them. They felt dismayed. But then, as they watched, the truck turned around. A young woman was driving and she stopped to get everybody on the truck. Ed sat in the cab with her. She honestly told him she had no intention of stopping, but then a voice told her to turn around and pick up these people. Ed thanked her, telling her she was "an angel in disguise."

At that, she got a bit flustered. She said to Ed, "Do you know what my name is?" and she told him, "My name is Gabriel."

Indeed, she was an angel, and she gave a very practical gift to people in trouble, stranded in a storm.

∞ ∞ ∞ ∞

Visitors to the beautiful city of Montreal in Canada can't help but be aware of a holy place on a hill called Mount Royal that is named St. Joseph's Oratory. A very holy man named Brother André, who was born near Montreal in 1845 and lived to be ninety, is recognized as the founder of this place of prayer. He was a simple, uneducated brother in the Congregation of the Holy Cross, who was deeply devoted to St. Joseph. In his lifetime, he was acclaimed as a healer and many miracles are said to have occurred through this man's faith. He balked at getting personal credit for these healings, and always insisted that it was the power of God at work because of the intercession of St. Joseph. On May 23, 1982, Pope John Paul II formally declared Brother André Bessette, "Blessed."

It was Brother André's dream to have an oratory dedicated to St. Joseph, and, toward the end of the last century, he had started to cast his sights on a tract of land on the western slope of Mount Royal, adjacent to the school run by the Congregation. However, this heavily wooded slope had been sold in the mid-1890s to a man named Michael Guerin, who was openly hostile to the school, the boys, and the Congregation. Guerin had put the land up for sale, but refused to even consider an offer from the Congregation of the Holy Cross.

Brother André and his superior, Father Geoffrion, were trusting that St. Joseph would come to their aid and let them get the land. Biographer C. Bernard Ruffin writes that they were more encouraged when another member, Brother Alderic, told them that "whenever he left the statue of St. Joseph in his room, facing away from the mountain, he would return to find the image pointed towards Mount Royal." He added that Brother André then commented, "That's because St. Joseph wants to be honored there."

Mr. Ruffin continues: "One day Father Geoffrion and Brother André decided to brave Guerin's dogs and walk up the hillside to bury a medal of St. Joseph in the hollow of a large pine. The two men besought the saint to remove the obstacles to the purchase of the land. Their prayers were not in vain, for within days, Guerin changed his mind and sold the land to the Provincial Council [of the Congregation]."

It could be that this development, occurring immediately after the placing of the medal and prayers to St. Joseph, was only a synchronistic occurrence with a happy, practical result for the Congregation. Perhaps Guerin didn't have any other good offers and simply wanted to be done with the sale of land he no longer wanted. But Brother André never doubted that St. Joseph was behind the change of heart.

What is very interesting is that a new custom has recently developed involving sale of property. For several years now, people who want to sell their house have sometimes been advised to bury a statue of St. Joseph, facing the house, to assist them in finding a buyer. I first heard about this when I worked for *The Litchfield County Times*. A woman called, asking me to do a story about this. She had had her house on the market for months and months. Then someone told her about the St. Joseph custom. Excitedly, she told me she buried the statue, and, within a week, she had a buyer for the house!

I have no idea where this custom originated, but I wonder if it doesn't stem back to the St. Joseph medal story told by biographers of Blessed Brother André.

Chapter 8

When Simple Coincidences are Heartwarming Gifts

If you talk about coincidences as being links to Heaven or signs of the sacred on earth, some may think this means that these incidents have to be spectacular. Not true. Most of the coincidence stories I have collected in recent years actually turn out to be somewhat simple, perhaps almost insignificant to a nonbeliever. Yet, I have come to believe that the simpler the story, the more evidence that God is really at work in our world. No one needs to be convinced of the power of God if the miracle is a big one, immediately recognizable as defying the laws of nature. But that's not how miracles usually occur. What we can see are the simple surprises that have no ready explanation other than, maybe, "somebody up there likes us."

What else could account for the blessing given to Geraldine Bedwell and a friend of hers. As Geraldine wrote me:

I grew up with a girl in a small town in Pennsylvania. We had a close friendship until I left to teach in Wilmington, Delaware. Although we exchanged birthday and Christmas cards for years, we had little personal contact after we both married and became busy with our growing families.

Two years ago a teacher at an elementary school where I served as a substitute received an urgent call at 11:30 P.M. from my friend's daughter, who, expecting to reach me, had dialed a number that I had had years before in my former home in Newark, Delaware. By coincidence, my old number was the current one of my teacher-friend. The daughter expressed a desire to reach me because her mother, who was hospitalized with a terminal cancer, was calling out my name and asking to see me.

I sent my friend a plant and note of encouragement. Her daughter said she smiled when she read her the message and she died a short time later. Since her death, I have shared many memories with her daughter, who invited me to her wedding last year.

ക്ക ക്ക ക്ക ക്ക

My daughter Mary told me about a simple coincidence that not only warmed her heart, but boosted her ego. Mary has a beautiful soprano voice and was auditioning for a church singing job. She knew she would be given a sheet of music to sight-read, and she was somewhat unsure of how good her sight-reading would be. She began to pray that they would hand her a piece of music she knew so she wouldn't "make a fool" of herself, as she put it.

When Mary went up to audition and looked at the sheet music handed to her, she was overwhelmed. It was the piece she had been working on for a memorial service for her brother-in-law Eric, who had died a month earlier. It was "The King of Love My Shepherd Is, Whose Goodness Faileth Never." My daughter believes that her prayer was answered because "God's goodness never fails."

ക്ക ക്ക ക്ക ക്ക

Kathy Belby of New Jersey felt God's goodness one morning in 1992, when she was still a member of the Army Reserves and just had gotten the news that her mother had breast cancer.

She called me with the news on a Friday night before a drill weekend and I couldn't stop thinking about her as I went about my usual duties at the unit. Would she need chemotherapy and radiation? How would this affect her energetic, active personality, or worse yet, was it possible that breast cancer could take my mother's life?

On the post where my unit drilled, Mass was held at 8:30 A.M. and morning formation for the unit was at 8 A.M. Normally, after a few brief announcements during the formation, I had plenty of time to get to Mass. As luck would have it, on this particular weekend, formation started late and I was still in the front row, nervously eyeing my watch at 8:25. The priest was always punctual and Mass never lasted more than twenty-five minutes.

The commander began a formal award ceremony for a unit member and I stood as patiently as possible. There was no way I could leave the front of the formation discreetly, but I desperately needed to go to Mass. Even if left now, I would still miss the Gospel and the homily.

Suddenly, at a pause in the ceremony, I whispered to the First Sergeant, "I have to go!" I left my place in the front row and hustled to my car.

As I drove up to the chapel parking lot at 8:45, the priest himself pulled in behind me! He had been visiting patients in the hospital and was late for the first time ever. I would be able to attend the entire Mass, start to finish, on this day when I needed God more than ever.

∞ ∞ ∞ ∞

Gertrude Engel of Hawaii remembers praying a lot as a teenager in Canada during World War I. One of her prayers was that God would send her a good Catholic man who wanted to have at least six children. At Mass one Sunday, the bishop urged parishioners to invite servicemen and others to their homes "to keep them off the streets." To the family's surprise, her father brought home an American civilian working on the Alaska Highway.

Gertrude tells how it was "love at first sight" for both of them. Best of all it turned out that he was a devout Catholic. They were married before a year was over. "Now, after forty-eight happy years and nine wonderful children, I urge all young people to pray for a good Catholic partner with whom to spend their days." Gertrude knows when her father invited Ralph to their home, this was no coincidence. It was proof for her that "God listens and loves us dearly!"

czo czo czo czo

August Martorana, of St. Louis, Missouri, also believes that God answers prayers, especially those of a child. He wrote to tell me about his sister Marie, a recent widow, who planned to cut the grass in her backyard while she was babysitting her three-year-old grandson, Tony. It was one of those days when no matter how hard she yanked on the starter cord of her mower, nothing happened.

Exasperated after repeated attempts, Marie told her grandson to say a prayer to God to help her start the lawn mower. "Little Tony, without a word, got up, turned his back while making the Sign of the Cross, and piously, though stuttering, said, 'P-Please Jesus, l-let the m-mower start for my g-grandma.' Marie, touched by Tony's prayer, pulled on the cord and the mower sputtered and started as she wiped away tears of thanks."

Is coincidence an "answer to prayer"? "Absolutely!" writes August.

czo czo czo czo

Terry Quillan, a nurse from Greenwood, Indiana, had an experience she feels was really the Holy Spirit working in her life to benefit others. Terry, who is the mother of two, is married to a "very spiritual man, not a Catholic," and is very devoted to St. Thérèse and Our Lady. She suffers from the debilitating condition of being fatigued and sleepless, called narcolepsy. She got to a point of feeling overburdened by her sleepiness, when her friend Valerie, a nurse, who also suffered from sleep apnea, suggested they go to a small "storefront"

Pentecostal church that was conducting healing services. They decided to give it a try.

On the night they were to go to the church, the first setback was that Valerie's van broke down, so Terri's husband drove them, dropping them off at the church. They found it locked tight and totally dark. Puzzled, they decided to walk across the parking lot to a big building that was lit to call Mr. Quillan and get a ride back home. But then they noticed droves of well-dressed people going inside and they wondered if the church service had been moved to this bigger building. But when they got close to the building, they couldn't find their way. Then a lovely older woman came up to them and asked, "Are you here for the service?" They nodded and followed her up the stairs. She writes:

As it turned out, when we got upstairs, there was indeed a service [Terri wrote], but it was a praise and thanksgiving service and a dedication. Emmanuel House of Prayer—not the church we tried to get into, but one block behind it—had just moved to this bigger, nicer building. This was a service unlike any I'd ever attended. I could really feel God's presence.... I was especially touched when a teen gang member got up to talk about how the prayers of this church had helped him and how Christ had saved him.

The last person to get up was the lovely woman who had greeted them. She asked for prayers because she was experiencing a debilitating condition where she fell asleep all the time and couldn't even drive her car anymore!

Valerie and I looked at each other, stunned. We knew just why we were there. After the service we went up to the lady and told her that we thought we knew what her problem was. We explained sleep disorders to her and gave her the name of our neurologist. She hugged us both and left the building crying in joy and praising God's Holy Name.

This God-incidence served lots of purposes. It brought healing, I'm sure, to that lady. It taught me that God's power is evident in churches other than our own.... I realized that reaching out to believers of other faiths is indeed what God wants me to do. I also realized I'm not meant to be healed physically—at least not yet. Through my affliction, God is using me to minister to others. I no longer pray for a cure.

As for the series of coincidences, Terri believes that Valerie's van probably broke down so that they wouldn't be able to drive off once they found the church shut. As for why the church was shut, they had visited on the fourth Sunday, only to find out that services were on the third Sunday. She believes she was meant to learn what she did by attending that particular service at Emmanuel House and so God saw to it that she was there that night. It was heartwarming gift for her to forever remember.

ogo ogo ogo ogo

John McNamara of Mahopac, New York, has worked for many years in prison ministry, specifically with a group called REC, Residents Encounter Christ. A couple of years ago he was the director of a retreat on a November weekend at Greenhaven Correctional Center, a maximum security prison in New York State. It so happened that his son Timmy had gotten a job with a company in the business of removing asbestos from buildings, and, much to his surprise, they were to do this at Greenhaven prison.

"This was his first time in a prison facility," said John, in telling the story. "At break time, Timmy noticed an inmate watching them. He felt led to go speak to the man, and to break the ice, he mentioned REC and that his father had been here to lead a retreat. The inmate's name was Jim, and, when Timmy mentioned my name, he said, 'Yeah, I know your father. I was on the team with him.'" And he spoke very affirmingly about REC and especially about John.

John said he was moved when his son told him about this encounter at Greenhaven. He told me that he had asked the men in prison to pray for his son Timmy, who had been having some troubles because of a drinking problem. The inmates had assured him they would pray for him, and now one of them, Jim, could see that

Timmy was working, doing fine. He had no doubt let the other inmates on the REC retreat, who were praying for Timmy, know.

"It was quite a coincidence that Timmy's job would bring him to Greenhaven prison," said John, and that he would start talking to an inmate—out of all the hundreds there—who knew him. "I took this coincidence to be a confirmation to the men in prison that their prayers for Timmy were being answered."

ൠ ൠ ൠ ൠ

In September of 1996, a story I wrote about a white bird that was an answer to a prayer of mine after my son Peter's suicide, was published in *Guideposts* magazine. I had asked the Lord to send me a white bird so that I could see this as a sign that my son was happy and in heaven, and my prayer was answered. After the story was published, I received letters and calls from many people throughout the country who told me their own personal stories of pain, most of them parents who had suffered the loss of an adult child by suicide as I did. One letter especially touched me. It was from Linda Wiebe of Mission, British Columbia. She wrote to the magazine, asking them to forward the letter to me. This is her story:

I too have a son with a chemical imbalance who needed many years of tending. In his frustration and confusion, he has recently left home, leaving me sad and yearning for his peace of mind. Feeling myself powerless and associating my own situation with Antoinette's request in her plight, and intensely desiring an answer, I found myself saying, "Oh Jesus, I'd be delighted with a plain black feather."

I am a shut-in, and several small children in my neighborhood visit me from time to time. Within ten minutes of finishing reading the account of Antoinette and her triumphant answer of the white bird, there was a soft knocking at my door. The knocking continued as I floundered with my walker to get to the door. Perhaps it was a young child too short for the doorbell and not yet old enough to realize that one knock was adequate.

Sure enough, there at the door were two little sisters, one not quite two and the other about three and a half. In the hand of the little one was a ragged black feather, at that moment, the most beautiful feather I had ever seen!

Linda included a drawing of what she labeled "My Black Feather," and I admit I was touched. Some would say there had to be a logical explanation for why the tiny tots came to her door within minutes of her prayer of petition. Others would label this chance or coincidence. I believe it was the answer to a desperate mother's prayer, letting her know that God would always care for her son.

ঔ৯ ঔ৯ ঔ৯ ঔ৯

Stuart and Laura Brush of Connecticut told me of a coincidence that gave them great comfort. Like myself, they are parents who have suffered the loss of two sons, one by murder and the other by suicide. Both their sons are buried in Vermont. To add to their loss, a few years later their two dogs, Hanna and Willie, became terminally ill and they had to put them to sleep. They had them cremated and decided to take the ashes to Vermont and bury them where their two sons rest.

"After we buried them, we walked to the lilac tree planted in Dean's memory. Then we both noticed a branch on which were two fuzzy caterpillars. One was black, like Hanna, the other blonde, like Willie," said Stuart. Somehow this coincidence of the colors on caterpillars resting on Dean's tree made them curious, wondering if this was indeed a sign that pets, too, may be reunited with loved ones after death. It gave them the image of Dean romping again with the beloved pet dogs, and brought great comfort to them.

ঔ৯ ঔ৯ ঔ৯ ঔ৯

Mimi Klocko of Delaware went back to college after raising a family. In 1995, after her last college class, she stopped at the chapel, as was her daily custom, to pray. "It was a cloudy, gloomy day, and the chapel was dark. I looked at the impressive crucifix on the altar, and a prayer of thanks came from my heart. I said, in a loud whisper, 'Thank you, Jesus, for allowing me to reach my goal. I just know you've been there with me all the while.'

"At that moment," she went on, "all the lights on the altar went on. It took my breath away. I soon realized that this wasn't a miracle, because after a while I saw the little old maintenance man shuffling around. He had put the lights on." But Mimi told me she has often wondered if the fact that the lights went on just at the moment she said her prayer of thanksgiving could have been a mere coincidence. She likes to think it was a sign that Jesus was listening to her words and saying "yes." What really matters, Mimi affirms, is that this incident brought her a great feeling of comfort and joy.

Chapter 9

When Coincidence Affects a Person's or a Nation's Destiny

Sometimes we read the lives of great people in history and come across an incident that confounds us in its significance for individuals in their lifetimes or for generations to come. These are occurrences which seem to verify that God indeed has created each of us for a specific purpose, as the eminent Cardinal Newman wrote, and that God will see to it that we get the help we need to carry out the co-creating work assigned to us.

Consider what happened to St. Thomas à Becket, the twelfth-century Archbishop of Canterbury and a martyr, when he was an adolescent. He had been introduced to hunting and was pursuing a hawk. His hawk made a dive into the river to snag a duck and the teenager jumped into the water to claim ownership of his hawk. So focused was he on his hawk that he never noticed the swift undercurrent and immediately he was swept down the river directly into the path of a mill whose waterwheel was turning. It was a moment of terror, when suddenly, as the youth was almost to the wheel, it abruptly stopped— the future saint was saved.

Could it have been merely a coincidence that something happened at that moment to stop the mill's waterwheel? Or was it, in fact, God's hand that stopped the wheel so that young Tom could live to do the work that would be so sorely needed by the world?

༄ ༄ ༄ ༄

Another story tells of a coincidence in the life of St. John of the Cross that saved him from drowning when he was but five years old. He was at a lagoon at Fontiveros, where children often went to play. One of their games was a very popular one where each would throw a stick perpendicularly into the water in such a way that the stick would come back up, allowing the child to grab it again. Young John had been playing happily, when, after one throw, he leaned to retrieve his stick, lost his balance, and fell into the water. The story continues:

"When he was at the bottom of the water, he saw a very beautiful lady who stretched out her hand, but he was afraid to grasp it because his own was so muddy. He was about to drown when suddenly, on the bank, a peasant came forward bearing a pole in his hand, and with this pole, John was drawn from the water. Can anyone doubt that it was Our Lady who sent the peasant with the pole at precisely the right time?" asks Joan Carroll Cruz, who relates this story in her book, *Mysteries, Marvels, Miracles, in the Lives of the Saints.*

∞ ∞ ∞ ∞

Coincidences in the lives of many scientists have resulted in discoveries that led to astounding changes in how people would live their lives ever after. While Galileo was the first to publicly demonstrate a telescope in 1609, it was a Dutch optician named Hans Lipperhey who actually made the astounding discovery that distant objects could be made to appear near. It had happened simply by coincidence, when he happened to put a convex and a concave glass together, utterly surprising himself with the amazing result. Or was his hand pushed a bit by God, so that humans could now have an instrument through which they could study the heavens and bring the distant stars close to this earth?

∞ ∞ ∞ ∞

Everyone should remember the story of Isaac Newton, the seventeenth-century scientist who formulated the laws of gravity. We all heard in elementary school about how he had made his greatest discovery in the garden of his mother's home while on vacation. It wasn't unusual for him to sit in the garden, meditating. For that's the kind of mind he had, one that never stopped asking the "why" questions of nature. As he sat there, an apple fell from a nearby tree. You and I would say, "so what?" Newton pondered it as one would a riddle. And then, the light came. He saw a truth—that the law of the universe is the attraction of mass to mass, not confined to earth alone, but a principle that applies from planet to planet, star to star. It is this strange mutual attraction—the law of gravity—that keeps every particle of the universe where it belongs.

It took a long time before scholars and scientists accepted Newton's premises. Some concluded that he was implying there was no God. He answered his critics, saying, "The fact that the universe is so beautifully designed in accordance with such harmonious laws...must presuppose the existence of a Divine Wisdom, the hand of a Divine Creator."

Some people today question whether Newton ever really saw the apple fall. I choose to believe he did, and that the event was more than just coincidence. I think God was involved. Maybe God wanted to use Newton's eyes to open our eyes to how beautiful and orderly this created world is—perhaps to counteract the disorder and the fall that had tainted the world when an earlier apple was plucked from a tree.

ᆼᆼ ᆼᆼ ᆼᆼ ᆼᆼ

Another chapter in the science books we study in elementary school deals with photosynthesis—how light plays a crucial role in plant growth, and how green plants give off oxygen. But the initial discovery came about because of a coincidence. In the late eighteenth century, Joseph Priestly, an English clergyman, a political theorist, and physical scientist, made an accidental discovery. He had placed a burning candle under an inverted glass, watching it flicker and then die. For some reason or other, he did it again, only this time, he placed a sprig of mint in with the candle. Several days later, he happened to notice that the candle was still burning. He concluded that clearly the mint had something to do with this, but he had no idea why.

He passed this information on to a contemporary, scientist Jan Ingenhousz, who came to England, performed experiments, and concluded that plants grow by "correcting" air polluted by human and animal life, and that this operation takes place only in sunlight. It would be another twenty-five years before scientists would come to agree that plants take in carbon dioxide from the air and liberate oxygen, a crucial process for ongoing, mutual living. It was the oxygen being liberated from the mint sprig that kept Priestly's candle burning and became the first chapter in this great discovery about photosynthesis.

But it all began with what some would call an accidental fluke. I have often wondered what made Joseph Priestly put a sprig of mint under a glass with a lit candle, an action that opened the door to learning a hugely important scientific truth.

༺ ༺ ༺ ༺

It was also what many have called an accident that changed medicine. It happened on a day in 1895 when a German physicist named Wilhelm Roentgen was experimenting with electric current flow in a cathode-ray tube that resulted in what he thought was an unknown radiation affecting photographic plates, making very strange pictures indeed. Because he didn't really know what was going on and what he had done, Roentgen called the phenomenon "X-radiation," X being the mathematical symbol for the unknown.

While he was puzzled, the scientist was still sure he was on to something, especially after he began using his accidental method to photograph metal objects and realized he was looking at the interiors of these materials. When he photographed his wife's hand and saw her bones, he knew his "X-rays" were a scientific breakthrough beyond belief—the ability to actually see inside the human body without cutting it open.

Was it only by coincidence that on that November day in 1895 a scientist would be playing around with electric currents and come upon a discovery that would save millions of lives? Or was it God's way of saying the time had come for a new breakthrough in discovering the mysteries of creation?

୦ৡ০ ୦ৡ০ ୦ৡ০ ୦ৡ০

Most schoolchildren remember studying the saga of the Spanish Armada, the great fleet sent by Philip II, the King of Spain, to invade England in 1588. When Queen Elizabeth got word that the dreaded Armada was on its way, she put the English fleet under the command of Charles Howard and Sir Francis Drake. Her military and naval commander, Sir Walter Raleigh, was ordered to stay at court, planning fortifications and coastal defenses. It was Philip's plan to have the Armada cover an invasion of England by the Spanish Army in the Netherlands, under the command of the Duke of Parma. This was no little squabble. The future of European power—and which country would have the most of it—was at stake.

History has recorded that "the elements espoused the English cause." Early in the battles, the Spanish fleet was scattered by a sudden Atlantic gale. The Spaniards were further weakened because Parma's forces in the Netherlands had been attacked with a devastating illness, and his army had shrunk from thirty thousand to seventeen thousand men.

The Spanish fleet refitted itself and recommenced the battle. And again, nature took over, with the Armada battered by more severe storms resulting in heavy losses along the rocky coast of Ireland and Scotland. Parma's invasion of England had to be abandoned. The Spanish losses in this ten-day battle totaled sixty-three ships, while the English lost none.

Perhaps it was fate that determined the outcome of the Spanish Armada. The consequences were significant, changing the course of history. From this time on, Spain, which had been the greatest European power of the age, lost its prestige and never recovered as the top-ranking force in the world of that time. The defeat of the Armada saved England from invasion and the Dutch Republic from extinction. England accepted her victory, which the people attributed to heavenly intervention. The popular saying became, "God blew with the winds, and the enemy was scattered."

ა⁊ი ა⁊ი ა⁊ი ა⁊ი

American history is rich with stories relating how the destiny of our country and contributions of noted individuals have been related to an apparent coincidence. One of these tales involved George Washington when he was an aide-de-camp to General Edward Braddock during the French and Indian War. This was never a good relationship, since Washington saw great shortcomings in Braddock's insistence on using European methods for fighting an American war. In vain, Washington tried to point out that it was most sensible to fight as the Indians did, sheltered by rocks and trees. Braddock saw this as "sulking cowardice," and, when they suffered a surprise attack from the French and Indians, he ordered his men to meet the enemy marching in order, full face ahead.

Washington had no choice but to lead his men in battle, in formation, according to the orders of Braddock. He tried to keep his soldiers brave, even as he saw his army nearly annihilated. The battle ended in a disordered flight by those who had escaped death. "How Washington escaped alive from this massacre is one of the miracles of history. Three horses had been shot from under him. His uniform had been punctured with several bullet holes. But his body had received not a scratch," wrote biographers Henry and Dana Lee Thomas.

If ever there was a God-incidence, it would have to be this miraculous saving of George Washington, who had such a vital role to play in the next years, when this land would not settle for anything less than independence.

ა⁊ი ა⁊ი ა⁊ი ა⁊ი

The fate of our country was involved with another coincidence, this one during the Revolutionary War, when the *Bonhomme Richard,* a crippled ship captained by John Paul Jones, battled the enemy British ship, *Serapis.* So badly battered was the *Bonhomme Richard* that Captain Pearson of the *Serapis* called out to Captain Jones, "Are you ready to surrender?" His answer has come down in history—"No, I have not yet begun to fight."

But the way it looked at that moment, those words were just bravado—until what some historians call "a lucky chance" turned the tide. The two ships were close, and a Midshipman named Fanning was about to throw a grenade. He could see a triangular opening at the widest part of the *Serapis,* probably made by an earlier shot. He knew he could do a lot of damage if he could send a grenade through that opening, but with the ship swaying and the hole so small, it would take a miracle to be that precise. He tried once. No good. Twice. Still a failure. And then, on the third try, the grenade sailed right through the opening. The explosion that followed was a blast that was fatal for the *Serapis.* Captain Pearson surrendered, and the battle went down in history as "the greatest achievement in naval history."

The odds that a grenade could have been thrown through a small opening of a bobbing ship in the midst of chaos were probably akin to finding the proverbial needle in a haystack. Yet it was done, and some historians call this a "lucky accident." What happened that day was crucial to the destiny of our nation. Could it have been only an accident?

∞ ∞ ∞ ∞

It was a surprising coincidence that happened during the Civil War, a chance occurrence that saved the city of Washington from the march planned by General Robert E. Lee. The leader of the Southern forces had proved himself to be a powerful leader, using tactics that by midway into the war had bewildered the Union generals, who had been routed at Manassas and Richmond. Now he planned to march upon Washington. "But his plan was frustrated by one of those insignificant instances that produce some of the most significant events in history," write Henry and Dana Lee Thomas. "One of Lee's officers, in gathering up his effects as he was moving from one camp to another, forgot a single trifling item—a package of cigars wrapped in a piece of paper.

"But this wrapping paper happened to be a copy of Lee's plan for the capture of Washington. It fell into the hands of a Union officer, who promptly turned it over to General McClellan. And thus Washington was saved from Lee's invasion—by a handful of cigars."

တော တော တော တော

It was a coincidence during Christopher Columbus' fourth voyage to the New World that literally saved his men from starvation. This voyage that began in 1502 had been plagued with troubles from the start. Two of his four vessels had been wrecked by a gale at Santo Domingo and the other two were wrecked at Jamaica. He and his men were fortunately saved and Columbus managed to get some canoes so that he could get to Hispaniola to report his condition.

By now it was February of 1504. Some of the men were exhausted and fearful and refused to go with him, wanting instead to settle in Jamaica. Revolting against Columbus, these renegades got the Indians to side with them, getting them also to refuse to bring food and supplies to Columbus and the men who were loyal to him. The situation was desperate, but Columbus was not one to face defeat without a struggle. He suddenly realized that a total eclipse of the moon was imminent, predicted in the Astronomic Calendar of Regiomontanus to take place on February 29, 1504, and this gave him a strategy. Trusting that the Indians could be frightened by celestial signs, he told the Indians that if they did not provide food for his crew, the moon would lose its light.

His prediction came true. The Indians were so frightened that they brought Columbus and his men the food and supplies that they needed. By the end of June, Columbus, now only fifty-three but exhausted and ill, had a ship again and was able to leave Jamaica and return to Spain, where he died two years later.

Could it have been only by chance that a lunar eclipse was to happen just at a time when the lives of Columbus and his men were in danger? This famous explorer was a strange man, who made enemies, but certainly he was religious. Some biographers say his religious fervor bordered on mysticism. History books say that in the last few years of his life, Columbus had begun using a new signature instead of his own name, writing "XroFerens," which means "Christ-bearing." Perhaps the Lord did not want Columbus to die abandoned and despised in Jamaica and so provided the famous eclipse of the moon.

ॐ ॐ ॐ ॐ

Coincidences have also been linked to the destiny of individuals. Imagine being on a sailing expedition with a captain and crew that had bravely started out to discover a northeast passage to Asia, only to find your ship, yourself, and all aboard trapped in Arctic ice. That's what happened to a man named Gerrit de Veer, and he lived to write about this experience.

The year was 1596, and de Veer had joined the Dutch navigator Willem Barents in this adventure that went sour. They had started out in summer, but by September, in the waters of the far north, ice began to form rapidly, and almost overnight these men of the sea found themselves trapped, their ship stuck in the ice, completely immobilized. "We could not loose our ship, as at other times we had done, and also that it began to be winter, we tooke counsell together what we were best to doe, according to the time, that we might winter there and attend such adventure as God would send us," de Veer wrote.

Their predicament was very serious. The one fortunate thing they knew was that land was ahead, though it was barren and frozen. They knew they had to put up a shelter, "yet we had not much stuffe to make it withall," writes de Veer. All they could do was "commit ourselves unto the tuition of God, and to that end we went further into the Land."

To their shock and joy, "we found an *unexpected* comfort in our need," the explorer reported. By a remarkable coincidence, they came upon trees, roots and all, on the shore. As for how they got there, there was no way to tell. The one thing the seamen knew was that these trees had not grown in this frigid place.

It was "as if God had purposely sent them unto us and we were much comforted, being in good hope that God would shew us some further favor; for that wood served us not only to build our house, but also to burne, and serve us all the Winter long, otherwise, without all doubt, we had died there miserably with extreme cold...."

Certainly, it had to be fate that had dealt these sixteenth-century seamen a kind hand, making it possible for them to survive a winter in the Arctic.

∞ ∞ ∞ ∞

Individuals also experience coincidences that change their fate. In the early morning hours of a cold March 12, 1936, Frank Chase, a tavern keeper in New Milford, Connecticut, would have lost his life, but for a coincidence that resulted in getting him heroically rescued.

A combination of previously fallen heavy snow and heavy rain storms had caused the Housatonic River bordering the town to overflow its banks. Chase didn't realize how bad the situation was as he drove along Route 7, getting close to the town bridge he had to cross to get home. Then suddenly, he was caught in the surging flood, with his car stalled and sinking. He knew he had to get out of the car because it was quickly becoming submerged. His goal was to try to get to higher ground, but he was immediately swept off his feet by the rushing water and battered by floating ice and debris. Somehow Chase managed to swing himself up and onto a large cake of ice jammed against a small tree. He stood there, clinging to the tree, shouting for help.

Now, normally no one would have been out near the river bank at two in the morning. But several hundred feet away from the bridge, up the hill beyond the reach of the flood waters, crowds of people had gathered to see the "show." It was, after all, the worst flood in New Milford's history. Almost miraculously, one man heard this human cry. His name was Bruce Nearing, and he was a night watchman for the Southern New England Telephone Company. He got a fire truck to beam its searchlight in the direction of the cry, and they saw Chase. The man next to him at that moment was James Guilfoyle, who worked for the Connecticut Light and Power Company. He noticed that Chase was a short distance away from a telephone pole. He suggested that maybe someone could ride a telephone cable car along the wires and rescue the man that way.

Nearing knew John Steck, the New Milford construction foreman for the phone company. He called him right away. Responding immediately, Steck got the equipment he needed from the company garage near the bridge, climbed a fire ladder to the cable strand and adjusted the cable car. Now his perilous ride began as he tried to reach Chase, four poles away. Swaying in the driving wind and rain, with huge ice chunks crashing against the already leaning poles, Steck skillfully maneuvered the car out, as he occasionally glanced down at the swirling waters, now some ten feet deep.

At each of the poles, he had to adjust the cable car. As he got to the fourth pole, he threw a rope down to Chase, who was about forty feet away, telling him to tie it around his body and make his way over the ice jam to the telephone pole. Then he climbed down. One look at Chase, who weighed about two hundred pounds, and John Steck knew the cable car couldn't hold the two of them. Thinking quickly, he knotted the rope in such a way that it became a loop, where Chase could sit with his legs lifted out of the way of the crushing ice cakes, should the jam give way. Steck climbed the pole, secured the rope, and went back by the cable car to get help. No sooner was he on his way, then the ice jam gave way, uprooting the tree Chase had been clinging to. If Steck had not arrived when he did, the tavern keeper never would have lived that night.

When Steck got back to the first pole, he found some men had managed to get a boat to the edge of the flood waters. By now it was near daybreak, and they could see well enough to slide the boat over the ice and guide it to the place where Chase was safely tied. They brought him back to the high ground, hearing him say all the way, "That guy's got nerve, I'm telling you." As for Steck, an unassuming man, he shrugged off the hero-talk and, in these emergency conditions, reported immediately to work.

Was it by chance that someone would notice a telephone pole forty feet from a man hanging on to a tree, with rushing waters battering him in a life-threatening situation, and get the idea of a cable car rescue? And was it a coincidence that the man he was talking to worked for the telephone company and happened to know just the man who could accomplish such a feat? Or was it fate that Frank Chase was not meant to die that night?

The person who told me this story is Joseph Lillis, former town historian for New Milford. Joe thought it would be nice for people to remember what a hero John Steck was to take that hazardous cable ride, risking his own life to save another, as the sixtieth anniversary of this event was coming up on March 12, 1996. And why? Because Steck, alive and well, and now ninety-five, deserved to hear that he was not forgotten.

ᵒ༄ᵒ ᵒ༄ᵒ ᵒ༄ᵒ ᵒ༄ᵒ

Knowing Paul Waldmann's story, one has to be impressed with how sometimes it is a series of coincidences that change the destiny of a person. Anyone who had ever read the books, pamphlets, or magazine published by Liguorian would have felt the impact of his work, even if they never knew his name. For Paul, a convert to Catholicism, and his wife Florence came to work at Liguori in 1953, working in managing, marketing, and purchasing for more than four decades. Paul retired in 1993 at age eighty-three. Just before that he wrote his memoir, called *Richer Than a Millionaire, One Man's Journey to God*. It is the story of how a Jew in Austria managed to escape from the Nazis, get to America, meet and marry a beautiful Catholic woman, find God in the Catholic faith, accept the pain of burying his only child, and find a lasting home and a position with a Catholic publishing company.

When Paul first wrote to me, he said, "You asked for stories of coincidences/miracles. There are about a dozen of them in my life's story." And he lists some of these:

"My coworker's arrogance stopped me from finishing my suicide attempt." His name was Ernest. He was a schemer, conceited, and would show his disdain for Paul by looking at him with a sarcastic grin. In 1928, feeling depressed, hopeless, and that life had no meaning, Paul walked to the gas stove, opened the jet, and prepared to die. Many thoughts went through his mind, and then he saw it—Ernest's face, broadening into an amused grim as he heard the news of his death. As to why this would be the image he saw, who knows? But it startled Paul enough to know he couldn't give Ernest that much enjoyment, and so he shut off the jet!

"A man walking in front of me kept me from ending up in the Nazi death camp." This was 1938, when the Germans had taken over Austria—a dangerous time for Jews. Paul was on a street and just ahead of him was a young man. Suddenly an older man was also on the street, confronting the younger one, asking if he was a Jew. When he said yes, the older man told him to shut his mouth and get into a wagon, which Paul could see was across the street. At that moment, Paul was near the house of a friend named Eugene. Knowing he would be next to get arrested, he quickly disappeared through the doorway, and was saved.

"Our mailman happened to be on the same street as I was and probably saved my life by a simple act of kindness." The mailman had spotted Paul a half block away and, pretending that he had a letter for him, called him. Paul walked over to him and the mailman said, under his breath, "Stay home tomorrow. They'll be arresting as many Jews as they can find." Then in a loud voice, he said, "No, I don't have any mail for you today."

"An act of kindness on my part done to a stranger opened the door to America to me." It was a plea in an underground Jewish newspaper that caught Paul's eye. It read, "My cousin John lives in Chicago. Can you help me find his address?" Paul felt instantly that he had to help this man, who lived far out from the city and obviously could not get to the United States Consulate to look up his cousin's address in the Chicago phone book. So he decided to go to the U.S. Consulate in Vienna, which had placed phone books of many American cities at the disposal of the general public, and try to find the man's cousin.

Unfortunately, the cousin was not listed, and, disappointed, Paul was about to leave. But then, out of mere curiosity, he decided to see if there were any Waldmanns in Chicago. "I couldn't believe my eyes, there were dozens of them!" It struck him that he could write to some of them and ask if they were relatives. So he copied addresses of about ten Waldmanns with Jewish-sounding first names and sent letters to each of them.

A few months passed and he heard nothing. And then one day, the mailman came down the street, waving at him, calling out, "A letter from America!" Paul writes, "High in his hand he held that precious piece of paper that became my open door to freedom. One of the Chicago Waldmanns had set the wheels in motion. And that man was not a Jew!"

Paul mentions other "coincidences" that turned out to be pivotal incidents, changing his life: "A disgruntled union official sent me to the place where I found my wife—the one person for me on two continents; and, finally, my utter disgust with religion was my moment of salvation." He had been completely turned off by religion, and had openly declared to Florence, his fiancée, that he was through with all of it. He remembered his mind being an absolute void that evening. He was alone, getting ready for bed, when "a thought entered my mind. I use the term 'entered' because it was not my own thought. It came peacefully, slowly and very distinctly, as if someone placed the words before me—one at a time. It was unmistakable. It said, 'Of course, Christ is God. How could you ever doubt it?'

"At that moment, I not only believed Christ is God, I knew it—as clearly as I know that I am Paul Waldmann." It was a powerful moment of grace.

Filled with a peace and lightheartedness that he had not ever known before, Paul walked into the living room. The radio on a small table was on and a male voice began to sing, "Yours Is My Heart Alone." It struck Paul. "I sat down on the carpet in front of the radio, and in my heart I sang that song to Jesus Christ, my Adonai and my God."

This is a story of a man's life, a tale of how many coincidences were strung together in powerful ways that led him to his destiny. Paul doesn't attribute any of this to mere chance. For him, the explanation is simple—"He speaks, and I listen."

Chapter 10

G ood Luck Surprise Coincidences that Are Life-Changing

S o many times I have read about or listened to stories that reveal how an unexpected incident was a turning point in a person's life, putting them on a path that opened the way to a future work or career that made a difference in their lives and the lives of others. I think of a Hungarian named Joseph Pulitzer, an immigrant who came to America in 1864 at the age of seventeen with his parents to escape oppression in Europe and find freedom in this country. But a war was going on and the youth immediately enlisted in the Union Army. At the end of the war, he drifted for a while to find work, and ended up in St. Louis. He then studied law, passing the bar easily.

But this man couldn't get enough clients to make a living. He was handicapped in two ways—his speech, because of his heavy German accent, and his appearance. He was excessively thin and tall, with a small chin and a big nose that made him physically unattractive.

It just so happened that he was reading a German paper, the *Westliche Post,* in St. Louis one day in 1868 and saw there was an opening for a reporter. Desperate for a job, any job, he applied and to his surprise got hired. The other reporters thought of him as the "ugly duckling" of their staff, but it didn't take long before they could see he was the best ever to be hired by the paper. It seems that Joseph

Pulitzer had found himself. Journalism became his life blood.

He went on to become one of the first of the "newspaper barons," purchasing the *St. Louis Post Dispatch* and then the *New York World,* always stressing sound news coverage combined with crusades and creative stunts to win readers. A man devoted to freedom and peace, he insisted that his papers carry stories of human interest and editorially battle for the rights of people. He was known for his ethical journalistic creed—"Try to see the truth about friend or foe."

Before his death in 1911, this great newspaper man had endowed the Pulitzer School of Journalism at Columbia University to perpetuate what was so important to him, a democratic press. Each year the prestigious Pulitzer Prize singles out the best in journalism and other media fields.

Could it have been only a coincidence that Joseph Pulitzer, a lawyer, was reading the *Westliche Post* that day and answered the ad for a reporter? Or could it be that another force was at work, opening a destiny for a man who could bring direction, ethics, and heart to the crucial profession of journalism?

༄ ༄ ༄ ༄

Most American children are introduced in social studies classes to Jane Addams, the 1931 Nobel Peace Prize co-winner. We learn that this great woman, the founder of Hull House in Chicago, spent her life trying to change the conditions that keep the poor trapped in their poverty. But few ever get to hear what opened her eyes to the suffering caused by extreme poverty.

Jane Addams had planned originally to be a doctor. She had even entered the Women's Medical College in Philadelphia in 1881. Unfortunately, she developed a severe curvature of the spine which forced her to give up her medical studies. When her family physician advised her to take an extended trip to Europe for needed relaxation, the young, disappointed woman went to England.

One evening she was restless and decided to take a midnight ride through London on a sightseeing omnibus. This particular tour included a view of the East End, the poor section of the city. Unexpectedly, they came upon a huckster's wagon, where men and women in rags were haggling for the decayed leftovers of the day that the huckster was auctioning off. Jane Addams was in shock. She had never seen anything like this. In her own words, as she later wrote, "The final impression was not of ragged, tawdry clothing nor of pinched and sallow faces, but of myriad hands, empty, pathetic, nerveless, and work-worn, showing white in the uncertain light of the street, and clutching forward for food which was already unfit to eat."

That moment changed her life forever. What she had seen changed her heart.When Jane Addams got back to America, she began to work in earnest to create a new philosophy of social service. In Chicago, she opened the first "soup kitchen" for the hungry, and later her cause included working for the abolition of child labor, interracial justice, and the establishment of universal peace. When she died in 1935, fifty thousand people of all nationalities passed her coffin, tears in their eyes for this woman who had loved them all, spending her life to alleviate their suffering.

Jane Addams was a rich girl with a noble soul who probably would have done good work in her life even if she hadn't had that searing experience in London. But isn't it odd that a twenty-one-year-old woman would suddenly decide to take a midnight ride in a strange city on an omnibus, and wasn't it quite a coincidence of timing that they'd come upon a huckster's wagon at that hour, a visit that brought out the emaciated, hungry people of the slums? Was this just a chance encounter, or was it destiny, as a biographer put it: "A daughter of the rich, she had beheld suffering from the top of an omnibus. A sister of the poor, she would climb down from her height in order that she might alleviate some of this suffering. On that midnight tour of London, Jane Addams had joined the 'universal fellowship' of mankind."

ॐ ॐ ॐ ॐ

A similar story is told about the birth of Hale House, the New York City resource for saving sick and abandoned babies that was launched in 1969 by a woman called Mother Hale. It was a coincidence that led to its formation. Mrs. Hale's daughter Lorraine was driving on a Harlem street when she saw a woman seated on a crate with a baby in her lap. The woman was nodding in a drug trance and seemed to be about to drop the baby.

"In a great act of impetuousness, I got out of the car," Lorraine Hale recalled. "I lectured her and told her to take the baby to my mother."

Mother Hale nursed the child through withdrawal and told the mother there was no charge for the care. Word about this saving act of kindness spread quickly, and within six months, Mother Hale was caring for twenty-two drug-addicted babies. Her work has made a difference and she deserved the national praise she later received for being one of the nation's "thousand points of light."

∞ ∞ ∞ ∞

One of the most amazing coincidence stories I have encountered centers on the founding of a Benedictine Abbey for women and how it happened that its location would be Bethlehem, Connecticut. Many people have heard of this monastery, the Abbey of Regina Laudis (also already mentioned in this book), because in 1950 a movie was made about how it was founded four years earlier. The movie was called *Come To the Stable,* and starred Loretta Young and Celeste Holm as the two nuns who came to America from France with a mission. This was a highly fictionalized version of why Mother Benedict Duss and Mother Mary Aline Trilles de Warren had come to this country, but it did put attention on this new religious house set up in makeshift quarters in the hills of the obscure town of Bethlehem. You have to wonder, why Bethlehem?

The real story begins with Mother Benedict and is indeed a drama. Her name was Vera Duss and though she was an American, she lived in France with her mother and relatives from the time she was five. A brilliant student, she became a medical doctor, with an M.D. earned in 1936 from the University of Paris. She had a longing, however, for religious life, and in 1938 she was professed as a Benedictine at the Abbey of Jouarre in France, taking her perpetual vows in 1941, a time when France was almost completely under German occupation. At this stage of World War II, it was not a good time to be an American in Paris and Mother Benedict found herself being sought out by the Gestapo. She was well known in the village where the Abbey was located because she had worked as a physician helping the people, and so she had to go into hiding. It was a time that required much courage.

Then came the momentous day when the Americans rode up the streets of Jouarre. Mother Benedict managed, with some of the other nuns, to get to the monastery tower, where they looked down and saw armored vehicles. But Mother Benedict saw something on these tanks that brought her great joy—a white star and the American flag. At that moment, something stirred in her soul, compelling her to then and there respond to the Americans who had liberated them. She would do this by starting a monastery of contemplative Benedictine women in the United States.

Of course, Mother Benedict wasn't aware of the obstacles ahead if she tried to pursue this commitment. She had to get the approval of her Abbess, of the Papal Nuncio in France—who was then Archbishop Angelo Roncalli, the future pope John XXIII—and of the powers in Rome. She had to find money for the trip and sponsors in the United States to greet her and the companion who would travel with her. She also needed the approval of an American Bishop, to welcome her into his diocese. It was a formidable task.

Amazingly, she got the official church approvals she needed. But the major obstacles of money and sponsorship loomed with few possibilities in sight. As she worked on these problems, several of the Jouarre nuns, including Mother Frances, asked if they could eventually join her in America. Mother Benedict knew that in America, if she ever got there, she would need nuns who had a skill that would bring in money. Some of the nuns at the Abbey had been trained to do book binding, and so she suggested that Mother Frances ask the Abbess to send her to a book-binding studio she knew about in Paris where she could take some lessons.

This turned out to be a fortuitous suggestion. Mother Frances was by nature quite talkative and at the studio she began to tell about how some of the nuns were planning to go to America. By coincidence, it happened that one of the women there was very interested in all things Benedictine. Her name was Marcelle DeLore and she came from a very wealthy family.

Also by coincidence, Mlle. DeLore happened to have two friends in the United States who were both Benedictine Oblates. These two women, both artists, shared a home with separate studios in a small, rural town called Bethlehem in the state of Connecticut. Mlle. DeLore met with Mother Benedict, and, impressed with her story and moved by the fact that the nun had everything she needed to make the trip except sufficient money and sponsors to offer her hospitality in America, was determined to help. She wrote to her friends, Frances Delehanty and Lauren Ford, asking if they could provide a place for Mother Benedict and her companion to stay until they could make some contacts in the States. Lauren Ford responded by return mail and said she and Frances would be happy to meet the nuns at the dock in New York and drive them to their home in Bethlehem, where they would be welcome to stay as long as was necessary.

"It happened in the nick of time," Mother Benedict told me, admitting how astounded she was at the coincidence, which only proves how well things work when God wants something done. "Because Mlle. DeLore believed in the enterprise and provided our specific financial needs, we were about to proceed. All the while, from the time of the Liberation to then, I had hope, but also anguish, wondering, will it happen? Yet, I couldn't be perturbed. I was doing this not for myself, but for God."

As it turned out, Bethlehem became the permanent home of the fledgling foundation, given the blessing of the Bishop of Hartford, the late Archbishop Henry J. O'Brien. All this had happened solely because Mother Frances and Mlle. DeLore coincidentally crossed paths at the same time in the same place.

చాం చాం చాం చాం

In the many interviews I have done, I often find that it was a coincidental happening that led a person to a "break" or a piece of "good luck" that put him or her on the road to success.

Several times I have met with the fine Emmy Award-winning actor George Grizzard, who grew up in the nation's capital where his father worked as a chief accountant in the government's General Services Organization. He had gotten his first taste of the stage after high school when he worked in a summer amateur production and pondered studying drama in college. But his father thought he should be a lawyer, and "I tried," he once told me, shrugging his shoulders. But law was not for him, and so, after college he worked in an advertising agency.

But his heart wasn't in advertising either. It wasn't long before he had a fight with his boss and walked out. Somehow he was walking right past the newly opened Arena Stage. As he put it, "Coincidentally, the new group had a play coming up. I auditioned, and the following Tuesday, I was an actor. The timing was astounding." If he talked about the acclaim that has come his way, his credits on Broadway, in Hollywood, and on television would fill several pages. Because of a coincidence of timing, George Grizzard—still acclaimed for his starring role in TV's *The Adams Chronicles,* and most recently in Broadway's *A Delicate Balance*—was put suddenly on the path that he was destined for.

∞ ∞ ∞ ∞

The life of British-born Elizabeth Blackwell (1821-1910), who was the first woman in the United States to become a physician, always fascinated me, perhaps because I aspired to be a doctor in my youth and even completed pre-med studies in college. Even more impressive was the influence of her father, Samuel Blackwell, a man of faith who believed fiercely in the equality of all human beings: black, white, rich, poor, men, women, and even children. He was once heard to say about his independent-thinking daughter, "What difference does it make whether Elizabeth is a girl or a boy?" He also taught his children that "the heart must be educated." No wonder that in spite of the fact that his seven children were still quite young when he died, the Blackwell family became notable social reformers, ardent fighters in the abolitionist and female equality movements.

The Blackwell family was in financial crisis after the death of their father, and Elizabeth, now almost eighteen, joined two of her sisters in starting a school. Teaching was considered an acceptable profession for women, but Elizabeth never really liked it, and she became increasingly restless. "An incident occurred at this time, which was upsetting to Elizabeth, but which at the same time seemed to offer a suggestion," writes biographer Rachel Baker. She went to visit a friend of her mother's who was sick with a malignant disease and knew she was dying.

There was something about this woman that touched Elizabeth, especially when she said she believed if she had been treated by a woman physician, "perhaps my illness would have been better understood." She asked aloud, "Why can't women, who are always preoccupied with the care of the sick, become physicians?"

At this time, Elizabeth felt repelled by the thought of what medicine entailed, yet she was fascinated. The woman died soon after this talk, but not before extracting something of a promise from Elizabeth that she would look into becoming a doctor in order to reduce the humiliation and pain of women who needed medical care. If it had not been for this unlikely encounter, it is extremely unlikely that Elizabeth would even have thought about pursuing such a path, one that would be strewn with incredibly painful rejections, insults, and setbacks, all because she was a woman. But she succeeded, and she changed the future of medical practice. Was this only a chance occurrence, or did it happen by a greater design?

Two more coincidences seem to point out that Elizabeth had been truly called to a healing profession. One occurred when Elizabeth thought she would be a surgeon. Surprisingly, she developed a terrible eye disease contracted while caring for a sick, indigent child. This eliminated the possibility of surgery for her, redirecting her into medical ministration, strategic planning, and administration of the first hospital for women and children in New York City. She cared for the immigrant women and children living in misery, ignorance, and filth, learned to speak their languages, and spread the gospel of responsibility for the poor. Her medical work was always to have a solid and strong element of human service in it.

The other coincidence in Elizabeth's life came when she was in France. She was with a woman who led her into her parlor and told her she had a present for her. "Elizabeth stared, bewildered, into the face of a woman... then she understood. It was a lithograph picture of the first Elizabeth Blackwell, taken from a history of *sages-femmes celebres*. Elizabeth recalled that she had heard about this woman—remarkably her namesake—who, a little more than a hundred years before, had published a work on medical botany in two large folio volumes, in order to get her husband, a medical man, out of prison, where he was confined for debt. Isn't it strange that there would be two women of the same name pioneering the same profession a hundred years apart? It would take someone much more knowledgeable than I to try to explain this!

∽ ∽ ∽ ∽

Knute Rockne is a name well known to Americans, especially those who love sports. He was only three when his father left Norway and brought his family to America. From childhood on, Knute lived by his muscles, and was a natural when it came to sports. He desperately wanted to go to the University of Illinois because of their winning sports record, but he had no money. He was working, lugging mail at the Chicago Post Office to earn money in 1910, but he was also competing in track events. It so happened that he started talking to two men who had competed with him and they told him they were going to Notre Dame in the fall. They invited Knute to go with them. His response was, "Why, who ever heard of Notre Dame? They've never won a football game in their lives!" His companions said, maybe, but at least it would be easy to find employment on this campus.

Knute decided to give it a try, and the rest is American history. This

Norwegian Protestant, studying under Catholic priests, became a football legend before graduation. In 1913 he was captain of the team that played Army, which was then the supreme ruler of the football realm, and Notre Dame stunned the athletic world by winning. Under Knute Rockne, the South Benders revolutionized football and Knute's destiny became football at Notre Dame. When he died in a plane crash over Kansas in 1931, at the age of forty-three, Knute, who had become a convert to Catholicism, was renowned for scoring five undefeated seasons in his thirteen years as head football coach at Notre Dame.

But for a conversation with two competitors at a track meet, Knute Rockne might never have heard of Notre Dame. Was this a coincidence or another force that put him on a life-changing path and allowed him to make a difference in his chosen work?

Chapter 11

The Many Special Ways that Coincidences Connect Friends

I have before me a beautiful little book called *On Friendship, a Selection,* published back in 1966 by a company that probably only produced a few special little books, the Peter Pauper Press. It is full of quotes about friendship, uttered by well-known people. One of the quotes I particularly like is from Henry David Thoreau:

"The most I can do for my friend is simply to be his friend. I have no wealth to bestow on him. If he knows that I am happy in loving him, he will want no other reward. Is not friendship divine in this?" I think that states what most of us feel about the tender relationship known as friendship—that it is a gift given in freedom, no strings attached, that yet is powerfully binding because it resonates with love.

Certainly in my years of gathering coincidence stories, I have recognized how often apparently chance happenings have connected friends, often at crucial times. Father John O'Donohue, a priest, poet, and philosopher who lives in Ireland, has a view of friendship that comes from the ancient Celtic spirituality that perhaps sheds light on what accounts for the special attachment between friends. He writes:

"It is a great day in your life when your friend comes. It is unnerving sometimes when you look at your friend and remember how contingent and accidental your first meeting was. If you had not gone to that party or to that lecture, if you had not walked down that street, you would never have met. Now in the season of your friendship, it is unimaginable that this person would not have been part of your life. The contingency of the beginning of friendship seems to suggest that there is a providence that brings friends together. One should always give thanks for the gift of friendship...There is no such thing as just two friends together. There is always a third force between them...."

∞ ∞ ∞ ∞

I remember how moved I was by the power of friendship when I read a letter sent to me in April 1996 by Catherine Reilly of Michigan. She began by telling me she wanted "to share one of the most meaningful coincidences with which I have been blessed." As Catherine relates:

In May 1990, at the age of forty-three, I was diagnosed with stage two breast cancer. I was going through all the pre-op testing, doctors' appointments, etc., and hadn't really given in to the anger and the fear. One evening in late May, my husband had the opportunity to go out with a few friends. He had been at my side since I first received the news. I told him to go and enjoy himself.

After he left, I was really in a bad state. The emptiness of the house seemed overwhelming. I was feeling very sorry for myself and was giving in to the anger. I had asked two doctors the previous year what this lump was and both said it was nothing. I had had a mammography every year which revealed nothing. I did what I was supposed to do to protect myself. Now these same doctors were telling me I had cancer. The anger was becoming all consuming.

I thought to myself, I'll call Jane, a very close friend, and just chit-chat. What I really wanted was to unload all that I was feeling. Well, there was no answer and I thought to myself, I can't even talk to anyone. I started crying, which became uncontrollable. Then, the front doorbell rang. I felt it had to be a salesman, and on the way to the door I had every intention of giving this solicitor a piece of my mind, disturbing people at dinner time. As I opened the door, still sobbing, my friend's husband Bill was holding the screen door open, with Jane standing right behind him. He kind of pushed Jane through the door and I fell into her arms, still sobbing.

Jane held me for what seemed like an eternity. I finally calmed down and told her I had been trying to reach her. She told me that while I was calling her they were at evening Mass and rosary service, which they were offering up for my recovery. After they came out of Mass, Jane told Bill, "I want to go to Cathy." It's a twenty-five minute drive and the whole time they were driving they were praying for me.

As we sat in the kitchen, talking over a cup of tea, I let out all my fears and told them that I was praying that I could accept God's will, whatever it would be, but I was really hoping it would be recovery. I remember saying that if I wasn't going to survive, then at least I would be fortunate enough to have time to be able to say my good-byes and rectify any wrongs I might be harboring.

We talked for a couple of hours, me doing most of it, and while sitting there, I could see them draining and getting tired while I felt both a sense of physical strength and inner peace building within me. I believe that I received all their good health and inner strength. After they left, I thanked God profusely for his intercession and believed fully for the first time that I would survive or that God would give me the strength to endure whatever came my way.

I have been blessed with many coincidences which I really believe are God's messengers. This is the first time I have told a stranger this story and only God knows why He wants me to share it with you, but there is a reason. For me, coincidences are not inexplicable—they are just God's work being done by people.

∽ ∽ ∽ ∽

I felt God's work going on when Virginia Leary, a dear and cherished friend, was close to death from lung cancer. Virginia and I had worked together for thirteen years, and when she got the devastating diagnosis, our friendship moved to a deep level of love and concern that expressed itself in a communication that brought both of us surprising joy. She never kidded herself about the seriousness of her illness, but she never lost her sense of humor and her concern for the people in her life whom she loved so dearly. I learned so much from this friend of mine, who never complained, and to the end, she maintained her ability to laugh.

A few weeks before she died, in January of 1997, Virginia, who was in the New Milford Hospital in Connecticut, asked me if I thought the gates of heaven would be open for her, a Catholic who hadn't been too careful about keeping up with Mass and the sacraments. I told her I thought they'd be wide open for a good person like herself, who had a strong faith and not a streak of meanness in her. I was, of course, praying that she would have peace and consolation as the final days drew closer.

As we were talking, a priest from the New Milford parish of St. Francis Xavier walked into the room, stopping to speak to the woman who was in the other hospital bed, closed off by a curtain. I recognized Father Tim O'Brien because I had interviewed him. He is a lawyer, and had a very impressive position in a bank when he left to follow the call to the priesthood. I had written one of my syndicated columns about him. I had also sent him a little gift at Christmastime, a large medal of St. Francis Xavier, since the first parish he had been assigned to was named for this great saint. My son Paul had found the medal for me.

When Father Tim saw me, he walked over, apologizing that he had not yet sent me a thank you for the medal. I told him he didn't have to thank me. I was only interested in making sure he got to talk to Virginia. For the next half hour, we had a great time and a few laughs. When he left, Virginia said she wished she had met priests like him earlier in her life. It might have made a difference in her approach to the church.

That had been a Thursday, and on Monday Virginia called me and asked if I would call Father Tim for her. She wanted to talk to him.

She wondered if he would come to visit her, prepare her for the death she knew was coming, and maybe have a Mass in his church for her.

I was overjoyed. I had been praying for this grace. I called Father Tim immediately and was upset to learn that he was on vacation. I left an urgent message on his voice mail. He later told me that as soon as he listened to the tape, he went to see Virginia. This wonderful priest met with her—and everything Virginia needed was taken care of. She died the next day, very much at peace. Father Tim arranged, with Virginia's daughter and family, to have a beautiful Mass for her. He gave a warm and caring sermon, so very personal. It was amazing how much he had connected with her in the brief time he knew her.

I have often thought of these days, and how friendship was the center point of all that went on. It couldn't have been an accident that Father Tim walked into that hospital room when I was there. And because we were friends, something happened as we talked that brought Virginia into the friendship circle, touched her heart, and led her to ask Father Tim to help her prepare for her transition to the next world.

∽ ∽ ∽ ∽

Back in 1994, I interviewed writer Dominick Dunne for a feature in *The Litchfield County Times* and was impressed with his account of a coincidence that showed how deeply friends can be connected, even if they don't see each other for a long stretch. Mr. Dunne, who is best known for his coverage of celebrity crimes, had been telling me about the painful relationship he had with his father who physically and psychologically abused him. In his own words, he revealed, "I was beaten with straps, hangers, and riding crops ...to this day, I remain partially deaf from a blow to the ear when I was in fifth grade." As for why his father, a prominent heart surgeon, was so hostile to him, the abuse came, he said, because his father thought Dominick was "a sissy."

That label changed when his son received the Bronze Star after saving fellow soldiers during World War II's Battle of the Bulge.

Drafted when he turned eighteen, Mr. Dunne commented, "I was so young to be in those battles." He fought side by side with a buddy named Hank. "We were glued at the hip. They called us the Gold Dust twins. I never talked about the war until a few years ago," he said, "and then it was only because I had an amazing experience."

In one of those rare moments we call coincidence, Mr. Dunne happened to go into a coffee shop in New York City, and his wartime buddy happened to go into that same shop at the very same time.

"We started to cry. We hugged. We sat for hours and just talked. I called my kids that night and talked to them for the first time about being a boy at war. I felt relieved. It's not so good to bury heavy stuff inside," Mr. Dunne told me.

Meeting his Army buddy decades later in the same place at the same time could be described as chance. But it was a time for friends to reconnect and it had such purpose. So much necessary healing took place that night. Perhaps there is a better explanation, something to do with the power of friendship, that could account for this unexpected meeting. But we don't really know. All we can do with certainty is tell the stories.

ೞ ೞ ೞ ೞ

I met Bill and Stacy Kosmides of Glen Ridge, New Jersey, in Rome when I took a first trip ever to Italy with my daughter Margaret in May of 1997. We were with a group tour, and on our first night, we all were in a great Italian restaurant, having a get-together welcome dinner with about five courses, lively music from a flutist and guitarist, smiling waiters, and, of course, red Italian wine. Inevitably the question always comes up when you're with new people—"What do you do?" I said, "Write." Everybody laughed, because, I guess, everybody writes. I expanded, explaining I write for a living, and that I was now working hard to complete a book on coincidences.

At that Bill smiled and said, "I have a coincidence story for you—and it's true." I wasn't surprised. Everybody I talk to tells me they have a coincidence story. This was Bill's:

I was at an airport in Cleveland and I met this guy who was about my age. It turns out we both had been in the Army and we started telling war stories. I couldn't talk about the Army unless I talked about my buddies, and the one I cared most about was my roommate, Warren Ornstein, when we were both in the military academy at West Point from '52 to '54.

I hadn't seen him or talked about him in many years. And would you believe, at that precise moment, when I was telling this guy about Warren, who walks by us, but Warren—*at that very second!* Was this a coincidence or was this a coincidence!

Undoubtedly, this was, as Bill repeated, a coincidence. Yet, it also said something about the power of friendship. Bill and Warren could have been in the same airport at the same time and still never have crossed paths. I wonder what it was that made this longtime friend happen to walk by Bill just as his name was being spoken?

∞ ∞ ∞ ∞

The most touching story of the special ways that coincidences connect friends came to me from Charles Grosso, an inmate for the past seventeen years at Greenhaven Correctional Facility in Stormville, New York. I met Charlie in the fall of 1996 when I participated in a prison retreat there. He served as the altar boy at Mass. The story he told me goes back to 1989, when he was working as a yard porter. One day, the man who worked with the prisoners in the gym, a civilian we'll call Duane, told Charlie he had an urgent message for him. He said, "Charlie, we have to talk. Somebody out there loves you. Come see me."

Charlie got a pass and went to the gym. Duane then told him he had been visiting his fiancée in California and while there they went to church where they met a woman. They started a conversation and he mentioned Greenhaven. The woman, in surprise, said this was quite a coincidence because she had a brother at Greenhaven. "The woman was your sister Angie and I promised her we will pray together," Duane told Charlie. He gave him a Bible, and then did more. He got Charlie a job at the gym.

Most of the workers there were guys Charlie had seen before, except for one. This was Hernando Mendez, called Nando for short. He was from Colombia, spoke little English, and was serving fifteen years to life for drug possession. "I didn't know it at the time, but Nando would become the closest friend I ever had," Charlie told me.

All the gym workers were housed in A-block, except for Nando and Vinny, one of Charlie's friends. They were in Honor Block, which has privileges not found in the other housing units. Charlie had applied for Honor Block several years earlier, but because of a few infractions on his record, had been taken off the list. But Vinny kept telling him to apply again because a new coordinator was coming aboard "and records get messed up when jobs change." Charlie found his original application dated 1986, then wrote to the coordinator. He was called in a week later. "It seems the new coordinator wanted to verify my application and there was no record of it up front. I gave her my copy. She went to the back, returned, and said, 'Mr. Grosso, I'm sorry for your delay with placement to Honor Block.' She went on to say that since his was the oldest, he would be the next one to move into Honor Block.

As it happened, when Charlie moved in, he was two cells away from Nando. Their friendship really took off and one day Nando asked Charlie if he knew of his case. Nando had noticed that Charlie was going to the law library almost every night, wanting to learn so he could "fight" for his freedom. Nando desperately wanted help because he maintained he was innocent. When Charlie read the case, he was appalled, convinced that Nando should never have gone to jail. The young Colombian had been working later than usual that day and missed his ride home. A coworker, as a favor, asked two friends of his to take Nando home. The driver, unfortunately, did not completely stop at a stop sign and was pulled over by police. The men were ordered out and the police searched the car. Inside the glove compartment, they found two ounces of cocaine. The two men immediately told the police that Nando had nothing to do with the drugs, that he was just getting a lift back from work. He was arrested anyway.

Because of multiple complications, the case went to trial and the fact that Nando was just getting a ride home got lost in the legal arguments. The jury never heard the truth and Nando was convicted and sentenced.

After Charlie read everything about the case, he became tremendously empathetic toward Nando. He started working on the case, hoping to find a way to get Nando back in court. "Nando and I became inseparable. I met his family; he met my children; we all had visits together like one family. And then the worst news came. Immigration was going to deport him as soon as he completed his sentence. I couldn't believe it. I felt sad, especially for his mother, Lucy. She had worked so hard to get her children one by one to this country without being a burden or accepting handouts. Would this country break up a good family like that?"

Nando's family came for a visit and they were quiet and depressed. Charlie tried to convince them they would beat the immigration ruling. Nando didn't believe it. Somehow Charlie found himself saying, "You have to believe me. My birthday's coming and the [immigration] judge will give me this for a present." That night and many to follow, he knelt and prayed the rosary, always asking the Lord to let his birthday be joyful—by getting the news that Nando would not be deported.

But they still faced the major obstacle. The immigration judge had the power to decide against deporting him, but to reach that stage, a deportee must first be granted a 212C hearing, and the attorney general argued that the five years Nando had served barred him from receiving the 212C hearing. The judge agreed, but ordered him to put that in writing for the next court date. Nando's hopes dropped dramatically, but Charlie kept telling him to have faith and not give up. He also kept on praying for a birthday present of good news.

At the next court date, there was a surprise for Nando. The attorney general had taken what the judge ordered for granted and did not put his opposition in writing. The judge was so angry at this that she then ordered the 212C hearing. Charlie was overjoyed when he heard this news, which meant they could now go ahead with the appeal.

Finally all the papers were in order, showing that Nando had a perfect institutional record; letters of support came from the civilian staff, his family, and, of course, Charlie. Now it was waiting time, and the answer arrived thirty days later, shortly after Charlie's birthday. They were all smiling as Nando read the judge's twenty-two-page decision and his "order" that Nando would not be deported. Charlie took the papers and turned to the last page to find "Date Entered" for when the judge's decision was made. He smiled. The date when the judge entered the order was November 9, Charlie's birthday. As Charlie commented:

It was a joyful day after all. It couldn't have been a coincidence. The birthday gift for Nando arrived through the grace of God. When Duane came to me saying "somebody out there loves you," he should have said, "somebody up there loves you." With God's divine intervention, all the moves for Nando were made. I was picked to help him. Once I came to that realization, I knew Nando had more work ahead. Within a few weeks after the judge's decision, we applied for clemency to Governor George Pataki. Then, one year later, on December 25, 1996— the Joyful Mystery of the birth of Jesus—Governor Pataki granted pardons to seven inmates. One of those seven was Hernando Mendez. Nando is now a free man.

In looking back at all the happenings that took place leading up to his freedom, while some might call it coincidence or luck, I see this as God's work. From Duane's meeting my sister in another part of the country; from the message Duane had from her, which led me to work in the gym and meet Nando; to the mix-up in the Honor Block application; to the granting of the 212C hearing; to the decision being rendered on my birthday; to the seven clemency offers on Christmas. All I can add to this story is while I continue to be confined, a blanket of happiness covers me. In time, a sign will appear for me to go free. I will join my friend Nando when that happens. But if no sign ever appears, well, the events that did happen will carry me until I come face to face with God.

Chapter 12

Coincidences that Are a Sign of Answered Prayers

Back in the long gone days when I was a youngster in parochial school, the nuns used to tell us that God always answers prayers by either saying yes or no. I think that may have made us a little cynical. Life has taught me that God always answers prayers, but according to Divine wisdom, not ours, and that means often the response from above is obscure and full of mystery. If there is a meaning to the word "faith," it is to accept that mystery, believing in its goodness, even if we cannot understand it.

Yet, there are times when God does answer a prayer directly, but in a way that a skeptic would call just a coincidence. As for how God decides which prayers by whom are answered in direct response to a petition, neither I nor anyone on this earth knows. I somehow feel it may be because the Lord knows we need a special blessing at certain times in order to continue doing the work we need to do on earth. Or maybe an answered prayer is like a gold star in our book of life for having done a good job already.

ࠕ ࠕ ࠕ ࠕ

Mary Murray of Warwick, Rhode Island, believes an apparent coincidence was really an answer to prayer. She is another reader of my syndicated column who wrote to me after I invited people to share their coincidence stories. Mary's "coincidence" happened on July 25, 1987, a hot, humid Saturday. After going to Mass at St. Rose's Church in Warwick that day, Mary drove to the Kent County Memorial Hospital to visit her friend, Kay McDonald. She wrote:

> Kay was a very holy woman who had founded the Blue Army in Rhode Island several years earlier. Now she was quite ill in the hospital. I had taken her there on Thursday. On the way to the hospital, I kept thinking how I wished I could get a priest to go and give her his blessing, she wrote, explaining that the pastor of her church had just retired and the other priests who knew Kay would be busy preparing for the Saturday Mass. Also, the hospital chaplain wasn't there on Saturdays. It took me only about ten minutes to get to the hospital, but I kept praying Hail Mary's all the way for a priest.
>
> I took the elevator to the fifth floor. When I got off the elevator, I couldn't believe my eyes. Here was a priest, walking toward me! I was so stupefied that I said to him. "Excuse me, Father. Are you a Catholic priest?" He said yes, a retired priest, and asked if he could help me. I told him I had been praying about finding a priest to give Kay his blessing and I just couldn't believe that I actually met him as I arrived.
>
> I remember he said to me, "I don't consider these meetings coincidence. I consider them God-incidences." Father came with me and blessed Kay.

Kay was whisked into surgery that day and, while the surgery was successful, her heart gave out and she died three days later. But meeting that priest in the hospital gave Mary "a tremendous sense of peace, knowing that Kay was in God's hands."

"There may be nothing to occurrences such as these, some would say. But don't you believe it for a minute. They are truly God-incidences and they happen all the time," wrote Mary, adding, "God bless you for making us contemplate this manifestation of God's loving presence."

☙ ☙ ☙ ☙

Tug's story came to me through a phone call after he read a story I had written for *Guideposts* magazine called "The White Bird from Heaven." He had his own white bird encounter and it was an answer to prayer. While he didn't want me to use his full name, he did want his story told, because what happened to him, he says, "helped save" him. He recalls that on a July night in 1992, he had been driving when he suddenly stopped on the road, walked out of his vehicle, looked around, and found himself praying. He was not a religious man. In fact, he only occasionally prayed. But that night, he was praying and his petition was a plea—if there is a God, please give me a sign. "It wasn't that I was going through any emergency," said this Indiana man, "but I did sincerely pray."

The next morning he got up to work on the farm, and suddenly there was a white bird flying by him. He had never, ever seen a white bird in the area where he lived, and has never again seen one since that day. But that morning, the dove was there, flying circles around him.

"It scared me, and I swatted at it. I thought maybe it had rabies or something. Then it flew up and landed on the peak of the trailer I had on the grounds, just looking at me. It just stayed there a while, watching me. Later, when I walked back up to the house, it flew right along with me, and stayed on top of a nearby shed. I got my mom Minnie to come out. She saw it staring at me.

"It was not until later in the day that I remembered I had asked for a sign that there is a God. Sometime later, while reading my Bible, my eyes fell on Matthew 3, verse 16, that says of Jesus: And he saw the Spirit of God descending like a dove and lighting upon him, and a voice from heaven said, 'This is my beloved Son, in whom I am well pleased.'"

A month later Tug's wife was diagnosed with breast cancer, and he believes she is making a fine recovery now because of prayer, something he would not have considered before the visit of the white dove. To this day, he ponders, "Could it have been a coincidence? What are the mathematical odds that a white bird would show up, hang around me a whole day, and then disappear forever?" Tug has no doubt that God sent the dove in answer to his prayers.

∞ ∞ ∞ ∞

One of my pleasures in life is reading biographies of great people. One who touched me is the scientist who established the germ theory in animal and human diseases and introduced the process we call "pasteurization"—Louis Pasteur. He was a splendid man who had great empathy for others. He hated war and injustice and was inspired by compassionate people like St. Vincent de Paul who believed that service to humanity is a service to God. Pasteur's own creed was beautifully expressed: "...I see everywhere the inevitable expression of the Infinite in the world; through it the supernatural is at the bottom of every heart..." When he died on September 28, 1895, one of his hands rested in his wife's hand and the other held a crucifix.

Because of his beliefs I have always felt that a major happening in his life, which could be called a coincidence, was more likely an answer to prayer. It occurred during the 1870–72 Franco-Prussian War, a disaster opposed by Pasteur, who called war the "massacre of two nations." He was forty-eight at the time and the war went badly for the French. He and his wife Marie were terribly concerned for their son, who had enlisted in the French army and was fighting under General Bourbaki. When the news came that Bourbaki had been disastrously defeated and that his men were scattered in retreat, trying to save themselves from being slaughtered by the Germans, the Pasteurs did a remarkable thing out of love for their son. They found a half broken down old cart, the only vehicle available, and the two of them, accompanied by their daughter, set out to try to find their son.

It must have seemed like a hopeless task. The roads were full of soldiers from the various regiments in tattered clothing, begging for bread. When the Pasteurs tried to get information about General Bourbaki's regiment, they were told that out of the twelve hundred men he had, there were maybe three hundred still alive. I can't prove it, but I believe this devoted family was doing a lot of praying as they searched among the devastated soldiers for their loved one. For amazingly, they found their son.

As their cart limped into a place called Pontarlier, they saw yet another soldier stumbling by them on the road. Mme. Pasteur shouted out her son's name, asking the soldier if he had seen him.

The biographer relates that the ragged soldier responded, "Sergeant Pasteur? Yes, he is alive; I slept by him last night at Chaffois. He has remained behind; he is ill...."

The Pasteurs started again on the road, I'm sure with much anxious prayer. They were barely out of Pontarlier, when a rough cart came rumbling over the frozen road. In it, lying on a pile of straw, covered with a ragged coat, was a soldier. It was their son. The family was so filled with gratitude and emotion, they couldn't say a word, but only embraced. With the love of the family, the son recovered from his wounds, rejoined his regiment, and survived the war.

It could be argued that the Pasteurs found their son by chance. But I have read this segment of Pasteur's biography many times and always am convinced that the Pasteurs' quest had a happy ending because God looked down on them, saw this as a love story in action, and was pleased.

∞ ∞ ∞ ∞

There's a church called St. Peter's on Barclay Street in lower Manhattan that is revered by many because of a man who used to worship there in the first half of the nineteenth century. His name was Pierre Toussaint, and, in 1997, Pope John Paul II decreed this black man, born a slave in Haiti in 1766, to be "venerable." Brought by the Berard family, his owners, to this country in his youth, after a slave insurrection against French rule erupted in Haiti, Pierre lived an exemplary life, working many years as a skilled hairdresser to support his owners. After gaining his freedom with the death of Madame Berard, he devoted his life to the welfare of others, buying the freedom of other slaves, supporting orphanages, finding shelter for homeless boys, and being wherever charity and love were needed. St. Peter's was his church, and he went to 6 A.M. Mass there every day for sixty years. Someone, writing about Pierre Toussaint, called him "God's image carved in ebony."

Now many people are promoting his cause for sainthood, chief among them Msgr. Robert O'Connell, pastor of St. Peter's. Now that Pierre is decreed "venerable," the next step is to be named "blessed," and that requires a certified miracle. Father Charles McTague, a priest of the Newark archdiocese and a former chaplain at Port Newark, believes his experience shows "a possible miraculous intercession" by Pierre Toussaint. Father McTague has been active in Pierre Toussaint's cause for over a half century. He is credited for doing the groundwork as a young seminarian fifty-six years ago that located Pierre's long lost burial place in the churchyard of Old St. Patrick's Cathedral in New York's Little Italy neighborhood.

According to a *Religious News* story, the "miraculous" incident took place in 1973, when Father McTague was assigned by Newark Archbishop Thomas A. Boland to serve on a forty-year-old rusty Dutch coaster converted to a radio ship and renamed the *Voice of Peace*. The ship was on a mission to patrol the Mediterranean waters off Egypt and Israel, broadcasting messages of peace. Unexpectedly, four hours out of New York, they ran into hurricane winds, with ocean waves soaring forty feet high. When a hole opened in the ship's hull and the pitching vessel began to take on water, the captain ordered the hole stuffed with rags and sealed with cement from a bag that had been mysteriously delivered to the ship just before sailing. It had not been ordered.

Father McTague recalled that the storm lasted six days and six nights. He was sure the devil was trying to sink them. His prayers for help were apparently directed to Pierre Toussaint to ask the Lord to save them. On the sixth night, the priest directed a steward to go to his cabin, remove a canister from his desk drawer, and empty its contents over the side. The canister contained earth from Pierre Toussaint's grave, which Father McTague had hoped to deliver to the ex-slave's ancestral West African homeland. It was a gesture of trust that Pierre would hear his petition and ask God to save them.

The storm didn't stop, "but a few minutes later, I saw a pinpoint of light," said Father McTague. "No one else could make it out until binoculars were used. It turned out to be St. David's light at St. Georges in Bermuda. We headed in for the safety of the harbor. We could not have lasted another day at sea."

The ship was far off course, and it could have been just plain good luck, or coincidence, that it had reached the Bermuda island. But Father McTague credits Pierre Toussaint for pointing the ship in the right direction and bringing them to safety. First, there was the matter of the bag of cement, mysteriously brought to the ship before sailing. Who was responsible for that? And then, it was almost immediately after asking Pierre Toussaint to guide them to safety, with the symbolic gesture of trusting this to his presence—by pouring dirt from his gravesite into the water—that they were brought to safety. While this probably would not be considered a certified miracle, as required for beatification, I would wager the men on that boat to this day thank the Lord—and Pierre Toussaint, who may have been listening to Father McTague—for their deliverance.

∞ ∞ ∞ ∞

One of the stories of a coincidence that seemed an answer to prayer that I have always loved stems back to the sixth century. It was an incident that occurred between St. Benedict, founder of the enduring religious order, the Benedictines, and his twin sister, St. Scholastica. The story is related in the biography of St. Benedict, written by St. Gregory the Great.

Apparently St. Scholastica used to visit her brother about once a year, staying in a house that was on the ground of the monastery, but quite separate from the monks' building. During her visit in the year 543, the twins met in the house and spent the day in prayer and discussion about things of God. Toward evening, as it began to grow dark, Benedict started to get ready to go. Scholastica, not coping well with the fact that he had to go—she missed her brother—begged him to stay the night with her. He said he couldn't, that he had to be back at his monastery.

Scholastica bent her head and started to pray. When she lifted her head, the sky, which had been clear, grew ominous with clouds; lightning started to flash and thunder roared. St. Benedict and the monks he had brought with him couldn't believe what was happening. The rain came down in torrents, and they knew they could not leave.

Benedict was not at all happy with this development. Feeling Scholastica had something to do with this sudden turn of events, he berated her, asking what she had done. "I prayed you to stay and you would not hear me," she answered. "I prayed to Almighty God and he heard me. Now, therefore, if you can go, go forth to the monastery and leave me."

According to St. Gregory, Benedict stayed, talking all night with Scholastica, "content in spiritual discourse of heavenly matters." In the morning, Scholastica began the return trip back to her convent— and she died three days later. Benedict died later that year and the brother and sister, both saints, are buried beside each other in the church of St. John the Baptist at Monte Cassino.

Some say this is just a story. But I feel that if it was true enough for St. Gregory to include it in his biography of Benedict, it's true enough for me to repeat! Again, some might simply say this was a sudden change of weather, something that frequently happens, and that it was a coincidence that it happened just as Scholastica was praying. What we do know, though, is that both saints saw this event as an answer to prayer, and their little tale has survived the centuries.

꿍 꿍 꿍 꿍

Ann Sobick of DeMotta, Indiana sent me a story that prompted her to ask, "Was this a coincidence or an answer to a prayer?

A nephew of mine died a dozen years ago at the age of twenty-nine as the result of choking on food. As tragic as a child's death is to a parent, more disturbing is the agony of wondering where that child is in eternity. It is easier to bear such a tragedy if you know for certain that your loved one is truly enjoying the presence of God.

My nephew had been dead for ten months when his birthday again arrived. The day before his coming birthday, I was doing some work in church. Stopping at Mary's altar, I suddenly asked my nephew to please let his mother know that he was in heaven.

The next day, as I arrived home for lunch, one of my sisters greeted me with the news that I won second place in a church drawing. This was great news, of course, especially as the amount was a good sum. But it soon dawned on me that some years earlier I had given my nephew a chance on a church drawing, and he had won second place. Now, after asking for proof that he was in heaven, on his birthday, I learned that I, too, had won second place in a church drawing. Was this a coincidence or the answer to a prayer?

For me, it was a clear message from my nephew to relate to his mother. What a great birthday gift he had sent to her. Maybe Mary had something to do with it. She certainly could empathize with the loss of a son.

Some could read this and think it was too trivial to be an answer to prayer. I don't believe that. I have lost two sons, and prayed often, asking them to give me signs that they are with the Lord in heaven. The responses are so very personal, that only I would be able to interpret them as an answer to my prayer. As one example, right after praying for such a sign one night, I woke up around 2 A.M., the hour that John had been murdered, because, in my bedroom, the smell of steak cooking on a barbecue was strong enough to rouse me from sleep. I got up from bed and went toward the kitchen, wondering if something was burning there. There was no smell at all as I left my bedroom. When I returned to my bedroom, the smell of the barbecue was even stronger than before. I smiled, knowing at that moment, how my boys had answered my prayers. They gave me a sign of something they would do together. Both of them were great outdoorsmen, and cooking on an open fire was their thing.

If I related this sign to others, some would laugh and tell me I have a great imagination. I imagine some would tell Ann the same thing for relating the "second prize" incident as a sign from her nephew. I really believe that our loved ones on the other side do respond to us, but in ways that usually can only be interpreted personally, linked to something only we know about them. Was Ann's coincidence an answer to prayer? I don't know for sure, but I would have to counter a skeptic with a simple question, "Why couldn't it be?"

০৯০ ০৯০ ০৯০ ০৯০

In April, 1997, the *Liguorian* magazine carried an article I wrote with the title, "Coincidences: Everyday Occurrences or Everyday Miracles?" Three months later, *Catholic Digest* reprinted that article. Richard Reece, the editor, does a kind of welcome note each month, greeting the readers with "Thoughts for the Journey." His July note began, "On page sixty-seven, there's an article I hope you'll find inspiring, Antoinette Bosco's 'Coincidences or Miracles?' As we go to press, I'm thinking of this article particularly because of a letter I received (coincidentally?) yesterday from a reader in Oregon. I'll call him Chris (not his real name)."

Rich went on to tell the story. It seems Chris, who lives on a ranch, felt the urge to pray out on his land one day, and so he got in his pick-up and began to talk to God. He actually said, "God I know you love me, but it would be nice sometimes if you would tell me so."

"Chris continued driving and meditating, stopping now and then to write his thoughts, until he was distracted by a coyote and forgot about writing and praying. Then something odd happened." He noticed a "shining gleam under a tree several hundred yards ahead." He stopped, got out of his pickup and walked over to see what it was. At first he thought it was a wad of tin foil, "but when I picked it up, I realized it was an old Mylar balloon that had floated in from who knows where.

"As I slowly unfolded it," Chris writes in his letter to *Catholic Digest,* "my heart raced. There, in large letters, were the words, 'I Love You,' surrounded by red roses. I don't know where that balloon came from, but I think God had the last word."

The people who have sent me their stories of answers to prayers that come in ways they could not have imagined, would no doubt say "amen" to that!

Chapter 13

Coincidences as Seen through the Eyes of Faith

Sometimes people experience coincidences which seem to them to have the direct hand of a Higher Power involved. These are incidents that can't be fully explained logically or scientifically. They leave the experiencers profoundly moved, believing they have been chosen for this special gift from what, they conclude, can only be a heavenly power. These are in the realm of the angel and miracle stories that are so popular these days. Many of these stories point to what we Catholics have always believed in—beings who have been assigned to help us, called Guardian Angels. The accounts that follow are true stories, told in the voices of the people who lived them. Their sincerity comes through so loud and clear that one can't help but be moved by the stories they relate.

☙ ☙ ☙ ☙

Sister Kathryn Ann Gunther of Dayton, Ohio, called her experience an "encounter with angels." It happened when she had arrived to attend a conference for nurses, social workers, and pastoral care staff members being held at the State House in Columbus. In her words:

Chaplain Nancy, who walked with me in the State House, offered to carry my purse. I have multiple sclerosis and at times find it rather difficult to carry anything heavy when I walk. Out of the corner of my eye, I thought I noticed a railing on the right wall. Without looking at the presumed support, I extended my right hand and grasped the supposed railing.

What a shock I experienced! The band on the railing I had grasped was moving faster than I could walk. Unfortunately, when I am afraid, my body becomes rigid. Suddenly I realized that the railing I had grasped was the banister to the down escalator. In less than a minute, my rigid body was stretched to its full length.

Then, as the railing made a curve to the right to become the banister of the down escalator, my lower trunk and legs rose quickly until my entire body was head-first on the banister. As I dug my fingernails into the moving band to try to secure myself, I glanced to the right and saw a drop of at least twenty feet to a rocky base with a tall, slender tree growing from it. On the left were the rapidly moving steps. I had no voice; I could not scream. I just knew that in a few minutes my head would hit the floor.

I heard Nancy scream, "Someone help us, she can't get down!" The next moment, I saw two men jump onto the escalator. When they touched me, I felt relaxed and released my hands to them. One of the men took one arm and the second man took the other. At the same time, a third man jumped onto the escalator from the top, lifting both my legs.

Gently I found myself carried off the escalator. The man who held my legs slowly lowered them to the floor while the other two men raised my upper body until I was standing erect, about five feet from the escalator.

None of them said a word to me. Evidently when they saw others ready to assist me, they faded or blended into the crowd milling about on the lower floor. They slipped away so silently that I couldn't get their names to thank them. As a matter of fact, I didn't even see their faces.

What was so remarkable about their transporting me from the escalator is my feeling no hand contact, no sensation of skin against skin, no discomfort. It seemed as if I were floating easily and comfortably while they lifted me from the banister and carried me to safety.

Without a doubt I knew that three angels had rescued me from the escalator.

When Sister Kathryn sent me her story, she pointed out that her friend Nancy maintains these were just young men, not angels, who merely happened by coincidence to be there when she needed help. But "God works through human beings," Sister Kathryn noted, and for her, the men who delivered her from a fatal fall will always be angels.

The popularity of angel stories has reached an all-time high, and numerous books and periodicals are now devoted to spreading the good news about heavenly companions who show up to help us in times of need. Sometimes it's good to recall that the subject of angels has been around for a very long time. St. Thomas Aquinas, the great scholar who wrote the *Summa Theologica,* included an impressive segment on angels—writing on their number and variety, their knowledge and love, and on angelic sanctity and, unfortunately, angelic sin, too.

St. Thomas' understanding of angels impressed me for many reasons, especially when he referred to them as our "angelic big brothers," and said they have much to teach us. The great intellectual master also wrote, "Some of them (angels) are friendly with that staunch friendship that endures, even heightens, throughout our weaknesses, our failures, our pettiness, our positive malice; so friendly as to be on guard for us twenty-four hours in the day." This is a positive affirmation of the belief that we all have guardian angels.

∽ ∽ ∽ ∽

Nelle Moffit Allen of Redford, Missouri, says she has always believed that she has a guardian angel, one she has kept very busy when she recalls the "list of accidents" that have happened to her since she was about five. Certainly, she was somewhat miraculously protected one day when she was careless in her kitchen. She writes:

I'm sure some of my stupid escapades keep my Angel wondering how much longer she will have to keep rescuing me. One of the dumbest tricks I ever pulled was when I had baked a pudding, took it out of the oven, and set it on top of the stove to cool. It had browned beautifully in a Pyrex dish I had used for years. I turned on a burner to cook potatoes. I was cutting the last of them up in a pan on the burner in front of my pudding when the Pyrex dish exploded like a gunshot.

I had turned on the back burner instead of the front one and hadn't noticed my luscious pudding was meeting such a doom, and me only six inches away from it. Long, sharp glass pieces flew in every direction, all over the stove, and burned holes in the kitchen tile. Huge jagged pieces had shot past me through the hall, clear into the bedroom, and burned the shag carpeting where every hot piece of glass hit.

How I kept from being ruined along with everything else is still a mystery and a very great miracle. If some had hit me, I'm certain they would have passed completely through my body, the force was so terrific, but not one sliver of glass was in my clothing so I never even got one small cut. It took me two hours to clean up the mess and longer to quit shaking.

Surely my guardian angel was watching over me...If she ever gives up on me, or goes on vacation, I'm a goner.

Many of the angel stories involve someone showing up to help with a problem that is not life-threatening—as was the case with Sister Kathryn—but simply one that puts someone in a miserable predicament. That's the kind of story Dick Sins of Erie, Pennsylvania, related to me. He was on I-90, a four-lane highway, pulled over with a flat tire. He had just bought the car and it only had seventeen thousand miles on it, so he didn't expect trouble. He had even more trouble when he discovered that the tire jack was broken and he had no way to change the tire.

Suddenly, out of the blue, a man in a black trench coat came walking toward him, holding a jack and telling him, "Here, I know your jack is broken." He handed the jack to Dick, and started walking away. "I asked him if he was going to wait till I change the tire so I could give him back his jack. He told me to keep it as he had no intention of using it," Dick said. The man was out of sight in no time, and as Dick later reflected on this incident, he could come to only one conclusion— "I had an angel experience on I-90."

ৎ৯৹ ৎ৯৹ ৎ৯৹ ৎ৯৹

The letter I received from Debbie DeJaegher of East Moline, Illinois, is a stunner. A mother of four children, Debbie related a story about an unexplainable happening that took place at a special home-Mass celebration for her oldest son's First Communion.

"I had baked a small loaf of regular, frozen, grocery store bread. It was to be just for Holy Communion. The meal afterward would consist of ham sandwiches on hamburger buns, with salad, etc.

"Before the Mass started, I sliced the small loaf and put it into a basket for the priest to distribute to everybody."

Since she was hostess for the fifteen adults and six children at the family event, when the meal was served, Debbie was the last to get a plate of food. She went to get a bun for her sandwich and to her surprise she saw that the bread basket, with two pieces of bread in it, was on the table, where it wasn't supposed to be. She looked then at the bun basket and, to her amazement, virtually all the buns she had put out were still there, uneaten.

"I asked my family what they had used for their sandwiches. Everybody told me, "Why the homemade bread!" But she had only baked a very small loaf, only enough for Communion. How could there have been bread in that basket after the Mass?

"I still marvel," Debbie wrote me, "after twenty-two years, at the 'miracle of the breaking of the bread!'"

Perhaps there's an explanation, but, like Debbie, I couldn't come up with one. Maybe someone by accident put the basket on the dining table and perhaps the Lord simply wanted to emphasize that for those who believe in the Bread of Life, the basket is always full.

ৎ৯৹ ৎ৯৹ ৎ৯৹ ৎ৯৹

Barbara Shook of Franklin, Pennsylvania, and I have been corresponding for several years now, ever since she wrote me a first letter, affirming, "God has surrounded me with angels and miracles." She has long worked as a volunteer in a cancer ward of a hospital, and she told me of a beautiful young woman she had come to love "as if she were one of my own. We shared so much. She told me her dreams and her hopes.When she was in the dying stage, her grandmother would say, 'Here comes Lisa's angel,' whenever I'd go into the room to see her."

Barbara went on, "Shortly after Lisa's death, I returned to do my volunteer work again. I started down the hallway and felt something stuck in my sandal. There in the bottom of my sandal was stuck a little gold angel pin. A very strange feeling came over me. I felt as if Lisa were telling me she was with the real angels. I felt I had been given an angel from an angel."

I was impressed with her story because my son Sterling had only a few days earlier told me his story about an angel pin.

Sterling has a serious heart condition. In March of 1991, his heart went into ventricular fibrillation, and, thank God, he received medical attention quickly enough to keep him alive. His heart has had to be monitored ever since, and the machine that does this is a "defibrillator," surgically inserted into his chest. Should he have a heart attack, this machine sends a shock through his heart and stabilizes it so it can return to normal beating.

Well, he and his wife Bernadette had been to a Saturday parish dinner dance to benefit brain-damaged kids, and he forgot to take his medication. Not only that, but they love to dance and were on the dance floor a lot. He knew he had overdone it when the defibrillator machine went off, sending 130 volts into his heart. He was frightened when it went off a second, and then a third time, jolting him with 750 volts. Figuring the shocks had stabilized his heart, he refused an ambulance to take him to the hospital, and went home instead.

Sterling and Bernadette say a rosary every night. When they got home, Sterling, knowing his heart was beating faster than it should, sat on the sofa with his rosary and, looking at a picture of Padre Pio, a man he is greatly devoted to, asked this holy advocate to help him be well. He also asked Padre Pio to send him one of his angels "so I know he was listening to me."

The next morning Sterling and Bernadette went to their parish church of St. Gregory in Tinley Park, Illinois, and, as they entered, noticed a visiting Franciscan priest, Father Gus, in the vestibule. Sterling had seen this priest before, but had never met him, so he went up to him to say, "glad to see you." Somehow, Padre Pio's name came up, and Father Gus said to Sterling, "I have a gift. I knew I'd give it away today, but I didn't know to whom." At that, he pinned something on Sterling's lapel. It was a little gold angel.

Sterling was speechless for a moment, and then he told Father Gus how he had asked Padro Pio for an angel the night before. The Franciscan, calling Padro Pio, "a friend of mine," smiled and said, "I like being a messenger for him."

Stories about how angel pins show up unexpectedly are not earth-shaking—unless, perhaps, they happen to you, as they did to Barbara and Sterling. But I have no doubt that for them these two stories present valid signs that we are indeed linked to the other world, even in such simple ways as being gifted with an angel pin.

৽৽ ৽৽ ৽৽ ৽৽

How strong a person's faith in God can be comes through loud and clear in the story sent to me by Hedy (she asks that I not use her last name), of Wallington, New Jersey. The incident she tells happened to her in 1974 while she was camping with her twin sister and brother-in-law at Algonquin State Park in Canada. In her words:

The second day, while hiking, I began running down a slope to catch up with my sister. My ankle hit a tree root, I lost my footing, and headed toward a two-foot-wide rock. I stumbled at a downward angle toward its center, picking up speed, unable to turn my head even slightly or raise my arm to shield my face. Feeling completely helpless, I cried aloud, "God, help me!"

Instantly, I felt a beam of light penetrate my head with the speed of lightning. It didn't hurt or scare me. And God's voice resonated outward from inside my head. He had the most beautiful voice I'd ever heard. His message was two-part: first, comforting—"Don't be afraid," and second, a statement, "You won't hit your head on that rock." He waited. I had to accept his words by faith before He would proceed. I immediately thought, "God does not lie!" Still facing the rock I was about to crash into, I no longer gave a second thought to my present circumstance. All of my being was now centered on God in complete faith. With that, God continued to be with me.

I now felt a circular motion travel around my body spiraling from my head to my toes, making my whole body limp. God then took my feet out from under me, and I lunged forward toward the rock, my arms at my side, my feet behind me. I slammed my right shoulder into the ground and slid forward, the impact forcing my eyes closed.

Shortly afterward, I felt soft grass beneath my cheek. Upon opening my eyes I was stunned to see that the jagged edge of the rock, which was now to my left, was less than one-fourth an inch from the tip of my nose. I now recalled how only two weeks earlier I had asked God to be "My Hero," and God had just now personally saved my life! I was deeply overwhelmed. Suddenly I felt my spirit burst within me, parting my closed mouth open with a great force—not of my doing—and I said in a loud whisper, "Praise be to God!"

My sister had seen the whole thing. She saw my hair strewn over the rock and believed I was dead. My brother-in-law, who rounded the bend above me, thought I had split my head open. In fact, all I suffered was a dislocated shoulder.

Only a year later could I tell my family what happened, and they believed me. I learned that God loves each of us dearly, is there for us, but will never force himself on us. We must seek him in all sincerity and complete faith. There is nothing God can't do, including intervening personally if it will serve his purpose. I deeply treasure this beautiful experience with God, who is and always will be my hero.

Someone reading this story without the eyes of faith could conclude that Hedy was just plain lucky, that it was merely by coincidence that she missed being crunched on the jagged rock by a hair. But I'm with Hedy and her explanation. In fact, she sent me her story, not to seek personal recognition, as she put it, sharing it "only so that others may know what God did for me so that God may be glorified."

ফ ফ ফ ফ

Carmen Rios of Elizabeth, New Jersey shared a story with me that also is a remarkable experience of how God helps those who have faith. Her story goes back to 1937, when she was sixteen and had just come to Manhattan from Spain. Her father had been working in this country and finally had a place on 106th Street so he could send for his family. She writes:

> From the very beginning we adapted beautifully to life in the city. My mother loved the big market running from 110th and Park Avenue to 116th. Her delight was to cook for the family. I went to school to learn the English language, and after a year I went to work. My first paycheck went to my grandmother, and from then on, regularly I wrote to her and we kept in close contact by letter.
>
> It was a cold morning when I headed for the station of the then-running elevated train on Third Avenue. I walked to the second platform about twenty steps from the local train. From this platform I could take the express train direct from 106th Street to 42nd Street. The train was a little late. I moved to the edge of the platform with my back to the track. As I leaned back to see if the train was coming, I lost my balance. Oh my God! I'm falling onto the tracks!
>
> At that precise moment, a strong gust of wind pushed me on my back and I regained my balance. I knew that the good Lord had saved me, and from my heart went a prayer of thanksgiving to heaven.

Both Hedy and Carmen had acknowledged their faith in God and I believe that's why they were rescued with God's love.

◌ೄ೦ ◌ೄ೦ ◌ೄ೦ ◌ೄ೦

My own daughter Mary also had an experience where she acknowledged God. And while she wasn't asking for help at that moment, we believe that God affirmed her expression of faith in a startling way.

Actually this was a trying time for Mary. She had graduated from Harvard's prestigious School of Business, and her M.B.A. had launched her into a promising career on Wall Street with a top-rated brokerage firm, Donaldson, Lufkin, and Jenrette. But Mary soon learned that Wall Street wasn't for her. She was in pain in her soul, in that difficult place where we all at one time or another find ourselves: trying to find a balance between our earthly and our spiritual lives. Most of the time we function more in darkness than in light as we try to reach out to God. But I have always believed that God is right there waiting to be seen and felt by us, if only we are receptive.

Mary wanted to believe that, too, but she was having a struggle. She finally found the courage to leave her high-paying position, and she moved in with me to stay while she made the transition from being a financial analyst to what she hoped to become, an opera singer. Her whole life was now in a state of uncertainty and at times she wondered and prayed to know—was she following her soul or only an impossible dream?

I was living in a rented house temporarily at the time and in the bedroom Mary was using there was a light fixture on the wall that never worked and apparently had been broken for a long time. I had called in an electrician and he said the problem was because the house was old. It would be too expensive to fix, he said, suggesting I live without that light. I agreed and bought a table lamp.

Then one night, we had a severe lightning storm, and Mary, in the dark, went to the window to watch the fireworks in the sky. As she relates it, she felt the magnitude and wonder of God so intensely in that moment it was as if the words were written across the black sky—"There's no question, there is a God."

At that moment, the wall lamp that never worked went on, flooding her room with light.

Perhaps there is a scientific explanation for why that happened, maybe to do with electrical currents. I'm sure some would call this merely a coincidence. But that doesn't matter. For Mary, it was a moment of grace, an awareness of God that doesn't come often to us. She saw this as an affirmation of the major decision she was making for her life.

Over the years, I have often talked with people who ask why God doesn't choose to appear more clearly to them. They want to have an experience, like Hedy's or Mary's, that takes away the uncertainty about God's existence and love and concern for us. To find God through faith alone is lonely and difficult, and, yes, full of uncertainties.

Yet, I think God is always there for us to see, only much of the time goes unrecognized. In our busyness, we get nearsightedly focused on the daily routines that must be carried out, and we inadvertently, perhaps, shut out the One who could help us make sense of all we do on earth. Sometimes it takes something as dramatic as a plunge down a slope, or a lightning storm to remind us of how much we are loved and cared for by the God who gave us life.

∞ ∞ ∞ ∞

In reading the life of the great composer George Frideric Handel, I have always believed that he was miraculously cured of a paralysis because he was a man of faith. If his father had had his way, George Frideric would have been a lawyer. George had a passion for music, but so adamant was his father that his son enter a profession where he could become financially secure, that he forbade him to touch a musical instrument. The boy, however, managed to hide a small clavichord in a garret, and after everybody went to sleep at night, he would steal up there and play.

When, at age seven, his father took him to the court of Saxe-Weissenfels, he slipped away to play on the church organ. He played "with such power and effect that the duke, who accidentally witnessed his performance, used his influence successfully with the father to permit him to follow his inclination," according to a biographer. He went on to have a prolific, but rocky career as a composer, especially having disastrous luck with operas, which left him fifty thousand in debt when he was fifty years old.

Things got worse that year. Handel was stricken with paralysis. He could not work and had to close the opera theater he had recently opened and declare himself bankrupt. He went to Aix-la-Chapelle where there were baths said to have healing waters, and he "was miraculously cured," wrote the noted music historian, Sigmund Spaeth. I would have to believe that the "miracle" came more from faith than the waters, because Handel then stopped writing unsuccessful operas, turning instead to composing religious music, his famous oratorios. The most famous of all, of course, is the majestic "The Messiah," written when he was fifty-seven and first played in London on April 13, 1742. Biographers write that Handel worked like one obsessed, composing this great work in three weeks. He never left his room in that time and once when a servant entered his room, he found Handel in tears. He is said to have cried out, "I did think I did see all Heaven before me, and the great God Himself!"

As for why the tradition of people rising for the "Hallelujah Chorus" began, Mr. Spaeth indicates this was probably due to a coincidence. He writes, "Some say that this was a mere accident, owing to the entrance of the King at that moment," which required people to rise out of respect for royalty.

Mr. Spaeth went on, "On April 6, 1759, Handel took part in his last 'Messiah'.... When they took him home, he expressed the wish to die on Good Friday, 'in the hope of rejoining the good God, my sweet Lord and Savior, on the day of His Resurrection.' Death actually came to him in the early morning hours of Saturday, April 14, almost as he had desired."

It would be impossible to believe that a coincidence could explain why Handel was healed at the baths at Aix-la-Chapelle. I think God still had work for this man to do, and it was to compose the music that would be played and sung by generations to come, music that would always lift people to sing of their joy in the Lord.

Chapter 14

Coincidences that Link Us to Deceased Loved Ones

I have always believed that we are in touch with our loved ones who have died. It was the beautiful teaching of the Communion of Saints that gave me this assuring sense that we are all connected to one another. But it was only after experiencing the deaths of loved ones that I had what I call "gifts" of feeling their presence. People I have met, who also suffered the loss of loved ones, tell me they, too, have felt the touch of that loved one from the other side, sometimes through a sign that seemed only coincidental at first.

Catholic author Mitch Finley did his own research on this subject. A few years ago, he placed an ad in newspapers asking for true stories of people who had experienced the presence of deceased loved ones, and he was amazed at the immediate response. People from all over the country wrote in to share their experiences, a collection of stories that became a book, *Whispers of Silence* (Crossroad). "Encounters with deceased relatives and friends are more common than one might think," Mitch concluded.

∞ ∞ ∞ ∞

People frequently share such stories with me. Frank Weller, a Catholic businessman who devotes much of his time and talent to helping others through such groups as Americares, told me of a friend he worked with as a hospital volunteer. She was Alicia Boyle, an Irish Catholic with six children, who had racked up nine hundred volunteer hours and was beloved by everybody. Sadly, she was going home from Holy Saturday Mass when she was struck down by a speeding car driven by an intoxicated man.

After the wake and the funeral, Frank went to the hospital, visiting some of the rooms where Alicia had met with patients. "I kept seeing how she had touched so many people in a deep way. I went from room to room and then left the hospital, depressed. I felt peculiarly alone. In my car, I turned on the radio and the first song I heard was 'You've Got a Friend,' sung by James Taylor. I felt it was a message from Alicia," Frank told me.

ক্ষ ক্ষ ক্ষ ক্ষ

As I was writing this chapter, I got a letter from Carolyn Haggerty of Eldon, Missouri. She told of her mother's illness before she died on August 18,1996, which also happened to be Carolyn's birthday. Her mother, very ill from cancer, had now developed pneumonia, but insisted nothing be given to her to prolong her life. "She was totally alert and we had to respect this," Carolyn wrote, adding:

> One evening as I sat alone with her, she asked me if I understood why she felt this way. She knew she was going to die from her cancer. I told her it made me very sad, but I did understand, and I added, "I only wish that you could let me know that you made it OK."
>
> After the funeral, a dear friend brought me a gift. It was an angel, which immediately made me think of my mother because it had patches and tears all over her gown and my mother always sewed clothing, made children's coats from adult coats, etc. For some reason, I turned the angel upside down, and there was writing on the bottom. It said, "For a good angel will go with him, his journey will be successful, and he will come home safe and sound."

Need I say anything more? My mother answered my prayers.

ᝍ᛭ ᝍ᛭ ᝍ᛭ ᝍ᛭

Another such experience was related to me by my friend, Frank Bianco. After his teenage son Michael died in a car accident, Frank went into near despair. He temporarily lost his faith, not being able to comprehend how God could have let this tragedy happen. It was during a visit to the Trappist monastery in Kentucky that Frank had a profound experience of "contact" with his son, a healing moment which enlightened him, filling him with a clear knowledge that God's love had always been with him and that his son was happy with the Lord in heaven. He went on to write a beautiful book about the Trappists, *Voices of Silence.*

Yet, from the time his son died, Frank found himself praying to him when he needed help, asking him to intercede. "It was uncanny. In life, if I needed someone to help, even in something simple like lifting the other end of a table, Mike would be there. There was wonderful synchronicity between us, and after his death, I still felt this," Frank related.

Never will he forget what happened one night on a mountain in Colorado. He had an assignment to write an article about two doctors who had become champion mountain bikers, and his destination was Durango, Colorado, where he was to meet them for the interview. He had decided to drive cross-country to get to the meeting place. To reach it he had to get up a steep mountain pass. As luck would have it, as he got close to the mountain, he started having trouble with his vehicle. It was now early evening and he pulled into a gas station, but the workers there couldn't help him. They just shook their heads when he said he was going up the mountain that night with a sputtering engine. But Frank was committed to being on time for the interview—which was set for seven in the morning—and he decided to take his chances.

As Frank tells his story, "As I drove up the mountain, I started going slower and slower. The engine kept 'missing,' and I knew I just wasn't going to make it. The mountain wasn't lit. There was no place to pull over. My van just started going slower and slower. I was in a predicament. I just started to pray to Mike, asking him to ask the Lord to help me."

What happened then is something Frank will never forget. The engine just stopped, but the vehicle kept moving. "I put my head out the window and listened. I couldn't hear a thing. I only knew that something was keeping my van going up that mountain. And I had a very strong sense of presence—that someone was with me. I believe it was Mike."

Frank made it to the interview, and was safe on the road until he was able to get to a garage to get the problem corrected. While some might speculate that the engine problem was not as severe as Frank thought, and that the van got up the mountain on its own, Frank would say, "No way!" He knows that his prayer was answered; the Lord had kept him safe.

ༀ ༀ ༀ ༀ

I related so strongly to Frank's experience because I, too, have suffered what I call the ultimate loss, the death of one's child. Two of my sons, Peter and John, have died, and I, like Frank, pray to them to intercede for me in asking help and comfort from the Lord. Several times, I have asked them to petition the Lord for me to give me a sign that they are happy and together in heaven. I have had responses, and while some may call these signs only coincidences, I know they are not, for I felt the touch of God in these instances.

In August 1995, I was preparing for the second anniversary of the death of my son John, who was murdered, along with his wife, Nancy. As the anniversary approached, I had been praying, specifically asking the Lord to use my son Peter—who died two years before John—to let me know once more that he and John are happy and together. As always, I asked the Lord to answer according to the Divine will, not mine. I was not seeking a miracle, only consolation.

Peter had died by suicide on March 18, 1991, a week before Easter, shortly before his twenty-eighth birthday. He was the light of my life, a brilliant achiever, who, in his own words, was "born with a missing part" that caused a chemical disorder in his brain. He struggled and achieved much in spite of his periodic psychotic turmoil, but eventually he could bear the pain no longer. He left us a tape and a note telling us it was "time to go home," and asking us to be happy for him because now "my pain is over."

On that Easter morning, a few days after Peter's death, I was awakened by a tapping at my bedroom window. There was a female cardinal, acting as if she were trying to get my attention. The bright red male cardinal, her mate, rested on a rhododendron branch. I felt as if the Lord had sent the bird to let me know that Peter was with him. I thanked God, as I fell to my knees, and thanked Peter, too.

In what I feel is not coincidence, but a "miracle," every day since then—for more than six years to date!—the lady cardinal has come to my bedroom window, always making herself known by the tapping. I don't need an alarm clock! And every day, this brings me joy because I feel she is a gift from God, representing Peter being in heaven.

Well, after my prayer to God on that second anniversary of the murders, to let me know if my two boys are together and happy, my lady cardinal came. But she was not alone. With her was another cardinal, not the bright red male, whom I have seen, but another female, like herself. I have never seen two female cardinals together, and certainly not on the same branch, by the same window. I felt overjoyed, and was convinced that the Lord had answered my prayer, letting me know that my boys are together, by sending me this sign of a second bird, like a clone of my faithful, daily visitor.

How could the coming of a second female cardinal on that day have been only a coincidence? I had never seen her before and I have never seen her since. I've always believed that nature itself is the constant sign that we are cushioned in Divine love-miracles—witness the stars, the sunrises, the sunsets. But sometimes the Lord gives us a little extra, more personal proof of this wondrous love—like a pair of lady cardinals.

I have another story I must tell that is related to this one because it, too, was in response to my prayer to God for another sign that my boys are together and happy in heaven. This happened on January 30, 1997, about six weeks before the sixth anniversary of Peter's death. I had gone to Fort Myers Beach in Florida for a much needed one week vacation and was staying at a place where there was a huge expanse of clean, light sand between the motel and the water. On the first day, as I walked the beach, I prayed and meditated, thinking of my boys, as I always do, while offering continuous prayers of praise, thanks, and glory to God, as I also always do. Then I asked again for a sign assuring me that Peter and John are always with me, humbly acknowledging that I really shouldn't be asking for yet another sign. Kind of in a lighthearted way, I admitted it would be difficult to get another sign that linked my two boys, since they were eleven years apart in age, but I prayed to God to let them come up with something, knowing they could come up with something much more innovative than I could think up.

The next morning, Friday, January 31, I walked the long stretch of white sand to get to the edge of the water. As I reached the place where the dry sand gives way to the sand hardened by the water, my foot hit something. I looked down. It was a small chunk of wood. I thought it was a strange item to be on the sand and stepped over it. But something made me stop, bend over, and pick it up. I thought of John, a furniture maker who so loved wood, and looked at it. It was indeed unusual, about an inch and a half thick. It fit perfectly in my hand, with my fingers sliding into wave-like ridges on its edges. I held it as I walked, praying as usual, again feeling my boys beside me.

I felt so very comfortable holding that chunk of wood. I felt as if I were holding a hand. After walking nearly a mile, I happened to take a closer look at the wood. I hadn't noticed before—but it was shaped like a diamond. Again, I thought, John would have had something nice to say about this piece of wood.

I was getting closer to the beach front of the place where I was staying when I felt Peter was smiling. And then I heard, clearly, as if he were talking to me—"Mom, don't you remember what you wrote in your book?" I stopped, my heart pounding. In that question, Peter had reminded me of something that hadn't crossed my mind at all, what I had written in *The Pummeled Heart:*

"After that horrible news—John and Nancy were killed on August 12, 1993—I used to look at my mother-ring. My six birth children had made it for me one year as a birthday present. My stone, the September sapphire, is large and in the center. Nicely arranged around it are two aquamarines for my two sons Paul and Frank, born in March; two amethysts for my two daughters, Mary and Margaret, both born in February; and my two diamonds, for my two sons, John and Peter, my April babies. I would stare at the ring and reflect on how my two diamonds are somewhere in the heavens, where they belong, with their Maker."

I had always referred to Peter and John as my "diamonds," and Peter was making me remember that. God had answered my prayer by letting my boys come up with a sign—their way, not mine—to let me know they are always with me.

I never would have dreamed up anything as imaginative as they did—a block of wood, diamond shaped, with finger spaces, so I could know they are holding my hand!

Again, some could call this a simple coincidence of a piece of wood, diamond-shaped, happening to be on the beach. But I believe even skeptics would have to wonder what the odds were that my foot would hit this palm-size chunk of light wood, the only solid object to be found on several acres of white sand?

And there's a footnote to this story. When I showed the wood-piece and related the tale of my answered prayer to my sister Jeannette, a professor at Skidmore College in upstate New York, she held the wooden diamond up in reverse. "Did you notice the back?" she asked, and answered, "an angel's wing?" That took me by surprise, for I hadn't really looked at the reverse side, but it clearly bears the appearance of an angel's wing! Truly, a prayer answered so quickly and directly can't be trivialized by being called a coincidence. I believe experiences like those given to me and Frank Bianco, and to so many others, bear witness to this.

∽∽ ∽∽ ∽∽ ∽∽

A heartwarming story about a widow's loneliness after her husband's death came from a woman in Wisconsin who asked me not to use her name. On Mother's Day, about three and a half years after her husband had died—a day which also happened to be her birthday—she felt a special need to know that he still loved her. After receiving Holy Communion that morning, she prayed to God to give her a sign to assure her of this. "I asked God, please, tell my husband I love him. But God, I am still here on earth and I need something I can see or hear or touch so I know my husband still loves me."

When she got home from church, the florist brought two bouquets of flowers to her door. One was from her daughter. The other said, "Love from Bill." Her dead husband's name was Bill! She started to cry and then went to the phone to call her son, figuring the flowers had to come from him.

Yes, he had sent the flowers, but he had put his own name on the card, not "Bill." To this day, the woman who wrote me said she doesn't know "why or how his name instead of my son's name was on the card, but I believe it was for a tangible answer to my prayer, telling me, yes, he still loves me. I have saved that card."

And this Wisconsin woman underscores the need to think twice before we relegate blessings to chance or coincidence, saying, "If we are more aware of things and more believing, we could identify many things that happen in our lives that show God's loving care for us."

ᑏᑏᑏ ᑏᑏᑏ ᑏᑏᑏ ᑏᑏᑏ

I have always believed that loved ones keep in touch with us from the other side, mostly through nature in some way, via birds, animals, flowers, weather, sky phenomena, and the like. After the deaths of my two sons, I had several experiences to affirm that. And over the years, I have had many letters from readers of my syndicated column telling me their unusual stories, most of them having a nature dimension.

One story I loved came from Gerri Yost of Sparton, Michigan and is about her mom, who had died at age seventy-eight, "after forty-three years of just plain hell with my father." Her parents had finally gotten a divorce fifteen years before her mother died, and in those years she had cultivated a beautiful garden and found peace. "In the divorce papers it was stated that if the property was ever sold, my father was to have first chance to buy it back. My daughter and I tearfully discussed how unhappy Mom would be if Dad ever got the land, lived in her house again, and walked in her garden. She didn't even want him at her funeral."

Gerri continues, "I am a farmer and my daughter was helping me pick tomatoes. It was a rainy day and as we picked, the sun started showing through on the west side of us even as it rained directly on us. After a while, I thought, 'we could have a rainbow.' So I stood up and looked toward the east. The sky was terribly dark over the woods—but a lovely bright rainbow was against the dark sky. I called it to my daughter's attention and we admired it for a few minutes before we bent down to harvest again.

"A little later I stood up, and to my utter amazement and disbelief, there was a perfect letter M sitting on the edge of the rainbow. My mother's name was Mabel! The letter was made perfect with pure white clouds. I whispered to my daughter to look and she stood there in awe. As we watched in total silence, the letter did not drift away. It gradually faded and was gone...." Somehow Gerri felt her mother was sending her a message.

That may be indeed what happened, for as Gerri then related, it turned out that her father didn't want to buy back the house, but "after what we had seen, it didn't matter." She felt at peace, and she knew that it came from the message she believed she had been given by her mother—that all would be well. And it was.

෴ ෴ ෴ ෴

Another beautiful rainbow story was sent to me by Claire Twitchell of Cotuit, Massachusetts. Her family was involved in a triple tragedy on Memorial Day weekend in May, 1994. Claire wrote: "My ex-son-in-law, his new wife, and my granddaughter, Rebecca, were killed instantly in a head-on crash in Plymouth. It was caused by a drunk driver who fled the scene and was missing for a few days. My grand-son, Oliver, was the sole survivor. My daughter, Terece Horton, the children's mother, was vacationing in Colorado, her first vacation away from them."

Claire's other daughter, Tara, gave the eulogy, an account of a "mir-acle," as the family saw it. Tara began:

My sister always called Rebecca her "rainbow girl" because ever since she was quite small, Rebecca loved to draw pictures of rainbows. She drew rainbows on Mother's Day cards, rainbows on Valentines, rainbows on paintings that she carried home from school. I remember once walking into Terece's kitchen and seeing a big picture of a rainbow that Rebecca had done stuck to the refrigerator door with a rainbow magnet.

Yesterday, on her way to her daughter's funeral, my sister closed her eyes and said a silent prayer to Rebecca. She asked Rebecca to help her find the strength to get through the ordeal ahead and she asked her also to please send her a sign to let her know that she was all right. Terece asked Rebecca to send her a rainbow.

Late yesterday afternoon, after my sister had left for the hos-pital to be with Oliver, it began to rain in Cotuit, where my par-ents' home is. It rained hard for a while and then, all at once, it stopped and the sun came out. My brother John was standing on the front porch, getting a bit of fresh air, when suddenly we heard him yell, "Hey everybody, there's a rainbow. There's a rainbow out here." We all came running out of the house. There, across the street from my parents' home, a rainbow had appeared out over the water.

Now Rebecca was never a child to do things in halfway mea-sures, and she also had a flair for the dramatic. This was the most magnificent rainbow I have ever seen. It was a great big wide band of colors that came down out of the clouds. Every color was represented, every color was vivid and bright, and the colors intensified as we watched.

What followed then was almost comical. Uncles leapt over hedges to get a better look; cousins ran out into the street without bothering to check for traffic; relatives were hugging one another; relatives were weeping; relatives were jumping up and down and cheering. I'm sure we must have looked like we had all lost our minds to anyone who happened to be passing by. But my family firmly believes that the Lord allowed Rebecca to send this rainbow to us to let us know that not only are she and Robin and Doug safe, but they are in a place that is more wonderful than any of us here can imagine. This rainbow was so beautiful it just had to have come from Heaven.

When the rainbow finally began to fade, and it took a while—Rebecca always liked to make sure she had made her point—I went back across the street into the house to call Terece at the hospital and tell her about the miraculous thing that had happened. When I did, there was a short silence on the other end of the line, then Terece said, "Tara, on my way to the hospital this afternoon, I stopped in Osterville at my office to pick up a few things. There, hanging in the sky, directly over my office, was a rainbow."

Claire ended her letter to me, writing, "I am aware of the horrendous tragedy you have been through with the murder of your son and daughter-in-law. I admire your courage and your faith. In spite of these 'crosses,' we have been blessed with the grace and strength we need to sustain us." I agree with her, absolutely.

ᑳᑲ ᑳᑲ ᑳᑲ ᑳᑲ

And I believe the Lord does gives us signs, though these may look like coincidences, that our loved ones are in heaven. I shall never forget the Sunday in August 1994, a year after my son John and his wife Nancy were murdered. I had gone to Mass at St. Peter's Church in Danbury, Connecticut, not my regular parish, because the Mass was at a more convenient hour. We were going to have a first anniversary memorial for John and Nancy and I had a crowd of family coming.

At some point during the Mass, I was kneeling and talking to my two sons who were with the Lord and I was asking them, "Was I right when I would tell you boys that 'Eye has not seen and ear has not heard what God has ready for those who love him'?" I repeated the question again, with my eyes closed.

I still feel in awe when I recall what happened at that moment— the cantor began to sing, "Eye has not seen and ear has not heard...," a beautiful hymn I had never before heard! The tears came running down my cheeks. I thanked the Lord for answering my question so quickly and in a way that had to get my attention.

I know others could say it was only by chance that the cantor was singing the very words that were on my silent tongue at that moment. But I know differently. This was another grace given to me by a loving God.

∽ ∽ ∽ ∽

Cindy Busch of Patch Grove, Wisconsin, sent me a story that could be titled "A Blessed Rose." In her words:

Our neighbor, Duane Hampton, lost his wonderful wife, Rita, in the spring of 1994. In losing her, we lost a great neighbor and my mother lost her best friend. My father had just had another stroke, and my mom looked to Rita for support and companionship.

Rita was a very special woman who never stopped doing for others. She quietly worked in her home, her neighborhood, and especially in her church, never seeking thanks or any recognition. She always did caring things for others and always had a smile and a kind word.

It was a shock when she died. Without warning, this special person was gone. My mother wrote a poem to her after her death. She attached this poem to a single rose for the wake and funeral. It made an impact on everyone attending because it summed up Rita's special ways.

In the days after Rita's death, flowers began blooming around Rita's home, flowers that Rita had planted and nurtured. A long hedge of roses was full of buds. One morning Duane looked out his window to see among the thousands of buds, one single rose, blooming, all alone. He felt Rita was with him. He shared this with us and took pictures of the single flower. It continued to be the only bloom for a week.

We all had a special peaceful feeling and felt it was a miracle, a special hello and goodbye from Rita.

∞ ∞ ∞ ∞

The mother-daughter bond was the connection I was told about by Phyllis Bergman of Dayton, Ohio. She told me how her mother, a French-Canadian immigrant, had grieved all her life for the baby who had choked to death on a chicken bone in soup, which was fed to her by a babysitter while her mother was at work. "In 1965, I lost my mother. I had the painful task of sorting through all of her possessions. In a trunk I found a clipping from a local newspaper listing my sister, Rose Maureen Zeller's death, 12-19-29. A chill permeated my whole being. I had held the hand, prayed, and said goodbye to the only relative I ever knew, my mother, as she died—on 12-19-65. Was this a coincidence?"

I would say no. It was a sign of the connection between mother and child, and perhaps a sign from the Lord that they would always be together.

∞ ∞ ∞ ∞

In his book, *Turn Your Hurts Into Healing*, Gilbert Beers, the former editor of *Christianity Today*, tells about his son Doug's tragic death in an accident. At the funeral service, Doug's cousins Tim Allen and his wife Jane, outstanding vocalists, sang a duet called "Finally Home." About four years after his son's death, Mr. Beers was driving home one afternoon, when he looked in his rearview mirror and saw a beige Volkswagen Rabbit. It was, he wrote, "identical to the car Doug drove when he died."

The next surprise was when he got a glimpse of the driver, a young man who looked so much like Doug, he could have been his twin. "Before I could recover from the shock, someone on the radio began to sing, 'Finally Home.' I am still stunned by the combination of these three," wrote this father.

Of course, some might call this coincidence, but any parent who has lost a child would know differently. When God sees the permanent pain of a grieving parent, God sometimes pours a grace and it lands right on the heart of the parent to give some moments of comfort and peace. I know; I've been there. God is not in heaven, but right here, in every bit of creation, side by side with us, and every so often, God lets us know we are not alone on this earth; we are not neglected and uncared for.

Yet, some stay blind to this loving care, remarking on the signs but only relegating them to "coincidence." As a popular saying puts it, "Coincidence is often a little miracle in which God has decided to remain anonymous."

Chapter 15

Reflections on Coincidence and Where Luck, Prayer, and Providence Come In

I was unprepared for the response I received whenever I would tell someone I was working on a book about coincidence. It was a subject that immediately raised interest and commentary, usually a verification that virtually everyone has experienced what we call coincidence: an unexpected, unexplainable incident that defies the way things are ordinarily supposed to happen.

Almost everyone would immediately mention "synchronicity" and Carl Jung. Jung, as most people know, was the noted Swiss psychologist/psychiatrist who coined that name for the phenomenon of what he called "meaningful coincidence." As explained by the coauthors of *Man and His Symbols*: "Dr. Jung put forward a new concept that he called 'synchronicity.' This term means a 'meaningful coincidence' of outer and inner events that are not themselves causally connected. The emphasis lies on the word 'meaningful.'

"If an aircraft crashed before my eyes as I am blowing my nose, this is a coincidence of events that has no meaning. It is simply a chance occurrence of a kind that happens all the time. But if I bought a blue frock and, by mistake, the shop delivered a black one on the day one of my near relatives died, this would be a meaningful coincidence. The two events are not causally related, but they are connected by the symbolic meaning our society gives to the color black." In other words, two events happen that are connected by their meaning, but they wouldn't make sense if you try to explain them as cause and effect. That's synchronicity.

Jung's premise is that "there are indications that at least a part of the psyche is not subject to the laws of space and time." In his famous essay, "Synchronicity, An Acausal Connecting Principle," Jung assumes there is "an inner unconscious knowledge that links a physical event with a psychic condition so that a certain event that appears 'accidental' or 'coincidental' can in fact be psychically meaningful." It is well accepted today that Jung was breaking new ground when he postulated his "synchronicity" conclusions.

What is sometimes overlooked in what I feel is a "sound bite" approach to Jung's concept of synchronicity is that the eminent psychologist saw this as a phenomenon that is outside of time and linked to the "numina," or divine spirit in all things. This is made clear in a letter Jung wrote to a friend—who had been asked by a monk named Korvin, Count of Krasinski—to give her an explanation of synchronicity. Jung wrote:

> ...Krasinski...forgets...that the most important cause of all things, i.e. God, Himself has no cause, and probably maintains a continuous creation with His eternal omnipresence. For this reason, all acausal events (that is, synchronicities, or meaningful coincidences) appear to be numinous...It is marvelous that it is just theological causality which does not allow God any free play. God must not only be exclusively good, over and above this He must also obey His own laws in creation. God is thus subordinated to the Church's apotropaeic tendency toward limiting His freedom.
>
> I do not think negatively of synchronicity as a mere absence of cause but...I also see it positively as a creative act which comes from the *ultimate acausal*....

Jung's Christian faith was one of the essential features of his life and his belief in God became more pronounced as he grew older. Five years before his death in 1957, he wrote, "I find that all my thoughts circle around God like the planets around the sun, and are as irresistibly attracted by Him. I would feel it to be the grossest sin if I were to oppose any resistance to this force." Yet, in all his scientific work, he seldom spoke of God, using the objective language of science and restricting himself for the most part to what he felt could be supported by evidence.

But stories are, in fact, evidence, as I have discovered in encountering the people, living and in history, who provided me with tales of incredible experiences. Jung came to his conclusions about synchronicity because of what he learned from patients and others, and from incidents in his own life. Even to the end, after his beloved wife Emma died, he found yet more proof for what he had discovered about meaningful coincidences.

As related by his biographer, Barbara Hannah: "...It was a very hard winter, with intense cold coming late; since the sap was already up in the trees, this led to the loss of many of them....The vine over the front door at the Tower produced a curious red sap which ran down over Jung's crest. He felt this was a strange synchronicity, so soon after Emma's death, as if the vine were weeping tears of blood."

ༀ ༀ ༀ ༀ

In her small book, *The Tao of Psychology, Synchronicity and the Self,* author Jean Shinoda Bolen, M.D., gives many explanations of the term coined by Jung. She writes, "Synchronicity is like a waking dream in which we experience the point of intersection of the timeless with time, where the possible union of spheres of existence is actual, and where what is inside of us and what is outside of us is unseparated."

Dr. Bolen points out that the best way to understand synchronicity is to have had a coincidence take place in your own life. "To fully appreciate what a synchronistic event is, one may need to personally experience an uncanny coincidence and feel a spontaneous emotional response—of chills up the spine, or awe or warmth—feelings that often accompany synchronicity. Ideally, there should be no way to account for the coincidence rationally or by pure chance." And Dr.

Bolen, a Jungian analyst, spells out the final gift of such an experience: "Synchronicity is the connecting principle...between our psyches and an external event, in which we feel an uncanny sense of inner and outer being linked. In the experience of a synchronistic event, instead of feeling ourselves to be separated and isolated entities in a vast world, we feel the connection to others and the universe at a deep and meaningful level."

I believe the people sharing their stories in this book would agree that the powerful effect of their coincidence is that they know now, in a radical new way, that we are not alone. Even St. Augustine, Father of the Church, in his sermons and writings preached of God's connections to us who are here on earth, so often seen as unexplainable events. He wrote, "I realized how many miracles were occurring in our own day and which were so like the miracles of old, and also how wrong it would be to allow the memory of these marvels of divine power to perish from among our people...."

In her book, *The Healing Power of Prayer*, Bridget Mary Meehan points out, "In Augustine's thinking, the world is sustained by the immanent power of God. When humankind began to take this marvelous reality of grace for granted, however, God broke through in a more unusual manner, using healings and miracles to draw people's attention to God's presence in the world." Many of these actions, which are signs of God's grace at work to get our attention, might well be called coincidences.

ॐ ॐ ॐ ॐ

What's extraordinarily interesting is that a book, *The Celestine Prophecy*, which became a leading bestseller in recent years, picked up on this same teaching of Augustine's—that there is a pattern or a guidance of people and the world toward a higher purpose, and that we can tap into this if we respond to grace. In an Author's Note at the beginning of the book, promoted as a novel, James Redfield says that "a new consciousness has been entering the human world, a new awareness that can only be called transcendent, spiritual.... It begins with a heightened perception of the way our lives move forward. We notice those chance events that occur at just the right moment, and bring forth just the right individuals, to suddenly send our lives in a new and important direction. Perhaps more than any other people in any other time, we intuit higher meaning in these mysterious happenings...."

The book is about an ancient manuscript found in South America that has ten insights about life's meaning, showing that we are guided by some "unexplained force." The "First Insight occurs when we become conscious of the *coincidences* in our lives" (italics by the author). When the entire culture begins to take these coincidences seriously, then all will wonder "what mysterious process underlies human life on this planet," Mr. Redfield writes, indicating as the book goes on, that if this happens, spiritual energy will be awakened and humankind will progress to an advanced stage of human evolution. But the first step is taking coincidences seriously, paying attention to what these are and what they mean.

I found that many sound theological and moral insights were lacking in the "insights" promoted in this book and for me it tended to be tedious reading. But I must be alone, since millions have bought the book and apparently found it inspiring. I have to say I applauded the author for highlighting the higher power behind coincidence and writing a book that is getting many, many people to focus on these mysterious happenings more seriously and to dig a little more deeply into what they may mean.

୦ଛୋ ୦ଛୋ ୦ଛୋ ୦ଛୋ

Many times I was asked during the period of my research how I explained the fact that coincidences are not always good. Some people pointed out that one could have a "God-incidence" that was painful, like being on a ski slope, hitting an obstacle you couldn't see, and breaking your leg. That could be called a coincidence, but not one you would be happy about. True, but some have come to believe that God is present in chance events, both disastrous and advantageous ones, and speaks through them both. Paul Pearsall, facing death, spoke of what he learned as he lay dying, in his fine book, *Making Miracles:*

> As difficult as it is to accept, crises are meaningful coincidences in our life as much as are the unexpected breakthroughs of joy. Meaningful miracles take place when we make them so; when we allow life's events—even illness and tragedy—to help us discover the oneness of our soul.
>
> I have never spoken with a patient, however sick, who has not felt that in some way his illness has presented him with the opportunity for a miracle. Perhaps a crisis has resulted in a rediscovered love; the forgiveness of a past transgression; a new view of what life means; an insight into the relative unimportance of local, mechanical living; or a new commitment to wellness.

This quote makes me think of my friend, Allia Zobel of Connecticut. She actually had that fall skiing on a mountain in Massachusetts, breaking her leg in three places, the tibia, the knee, and the ankle. It was a disaster, and then a funny thing happened on her way to healing, which took a year. She had the chance to do a lot of thinking, and she realized how unhappy she had been in her job, working for lawyers in litigation. She had always wanted to be a writer, and this crisis she was in catapulted her into changing her life. She began to write and before long hit the publishing world quite impressively, mainly with humor books, like *The Joy of Being Single.* Ironically, this book came out just before she found a fine man and got married. Her life became a "total awakening," and she was even led to return to the Catholic Church. One could ask, was the coincidence of Allia's disastrous fall on the slope a God-incidence? The answer may truly be yes.

∞ ∞ ∞ ∞

The Rev. Ronald Rolheiser, in his extraordinary book, *The Shattered Lantern,* makes the point that we must learn to see "the finger of God, divine providence, in all the events," both the blows and the gifts. He too tells a story of a woman who chose to skip Mass one Sunday morning and go skiing. On her first run down, she hit a tree and broke her leg.

The following Sunday, sporting a big cast, she went to Mass. A visiting priest gave the homily: "There is a custom among shepherds in Israel that existed at the time of Jesus and is still practiced today.... Sometimes very early on in the life of a lamb, a shepherd senses that it is going to be a congenital stray, one forever drifting away from the herd. What the shepherd does then is to take the lamb and deliberately break its leg so that he has to carry it until its leg is healed. By that time, the lamb has become so attached to the shepherd that it never strays again."

Father Rohlheiser goes on, "'I may be dense!'" concluded this woman, "'but given my broken leg and this chance coincidence, hearing this woke up something inside me. Fifteen years have passed since then, and I have prayed and gone to church regularly ever since.'

"What this woman experienced that Sunday was precisely the language of God, divine providence, God's finger in her life, through a conspiracy of accidents. In her response, she read the signs," writes Father Rohlheiser.

He goes on to point out, however, that today, such a concept of divine providence that sees God's benevolence even in events that deeply hurt "is not very popular." And the priest then urges that we always ask in whatever happens to us, coincidences included, "What is God saying to us in all of this?" and then we should seek to listen.

Paul Pearsall has learned something well worth thinking about because of his own personal pain. He says, "Each coincidence in your life provides you with a choice of whether or not to use that coincidence as a life lesson or to dismiss it as a statistical fluke."

∞ ∞ ∞ ∞

Donal Dorr, in his book, *Divine Energy, God Beyond Us, Within Us, Among Us,* underscores the importance of not dismissing the lessons of coincidences:

I find that when life is really "flowing" for me, everything seems to fall into place through a remarkable series of coincidences. On the other hand, when I am "out of sync" with life, many things seem to go wrong.... Suppose one accepts that coincidences are not always just random events but that they occur whenever a person succeeds in remaining in touch with "the flow of life." Such an acceptance has important implications. It opens up the prospect—and the challenge—of becoming more fully human by being deeply and consistently in tune with the nature world, and with the flow of energy between people. It means that the call to be human includes the development of an attitude and a spirituality which in some way promotes a flow of benign coincidences in life.

∽ ∽ ∽ ∽

Many people speak of how coincidences have a "connecting" principle. This is true when chance encounters bring two people together and a "flow of energy" ensues which initiates a very major impact on their lives. "This may not be of life-altering magnitude, but it decidedly adds richness to those who encounter one another for the better in unexpected ways," said a friend.

Pulitzer Prize-winning playwright Arthur Miller commented on this "connecting" principle in coincidences during an interview I was doing with him after his autobiography, *Timebends,* came out in 1988. He had included an incident about his mother, which happened one night when, out of a deep sleep, she suddenly sat up and said, "My mother died." He writes, "which she had, it turned out, and at approximately that hour of the night."

Then he told me about several other similar experiences he has had over the years:

I do put credence in that kind of connection. I think it's a sensitivity we have. We're not able to name it, let alone evoke it at will. It's a connection which is totally mysterious, but I'm convinced it does exist. It has happened to me about six times in the past year....One day I found myself wondering what had happened to someone I hadn't seen in fifteen years. That evening, he called up.... Inge [Miller's wife, photographer Inge Morath] and I were in Granada not long ago and I thought of a man, not a close friend, but again someone I hadn't seen in sixteen years, and on the way home, there's his widow on the plane.... I have suddenly confronted people I never laid eyes on before and knew their names....This is inexplicable, we only have so many senses—but maybe there are more.

ᓍᓬ ᓍᓬ ᓍᓬ ᓍᓬ

Another point of view on coincidences was offered to me by Chuck Vrtacek:

I have always thought of coincidences as conclusions. For whatever reason, wheels are set in motion and sometimes it takes a long time before the reverberations they set up are felt. I think of it sort of as a boomerang. You throw a boomerang, it goes out, turns around and comes back to where it started. I think coincidences somehow work this way. An action takes place in life and eventually comes full circle, back to where it started, though in some changed form.

I'm not sure I'm articulating this clearly, but my adoption and nursing school are a good example. I was born in Middletown, Connecticut, in 1953. That's like the throwing of the boomerang. Then my life takes its course. That's the boomerang going out and coming back. Finally, after all the things that could have happened to me, all the decisions and choices I could have made and all the places I could have lived, I end up going to nursing school forty years later in the same building I was born in. That's a coincidence! But it's also a completed cycle.

ᓍᓬ ᓍᓬ ᓍᓬ ᓍᓬ

Yet another point of view about coincidence comes from scientist

Arthur Koestler, who has more name recognition for his pro-freedom, anti-Communist book, *Darkness at Noon,* than for his scientific work. His language to describe coincidence in science was "bisociative patterns." In a 1964 article in *The Washington Post,* George Steiner writes of Koestler's view of the "creative unconscious":

> But what governs the timing of the intuitive shock? What made Pythagoras stop in front of a blacksmith's shop and note that metal rods of different lengths gave different sounds under the hammer....There is, says Koestler, a crucial readiness, a gathering of awareness at specific thresholds. Individual minds at various points in a culture become saturated with a problem. The unconscious worries at it like a terrier. Even while attention is relaxed or elsewhere—indeed, particularly then—the current of subterranean thought seeks its goal. Coming into the "field of readiness" a chance incident can act as release. Only if we assume such states of creative latency can we account for the undoubted fact that many scientific discoveries have been made more or less simultaneously by men who had no knowledge of each other's work. The gas was ready for the spark.

Koestler, who became known as a leading researcher of synchronicity after he wrote his book, *The Roots of Coincidence,* was clear in his concurrence about such events. In the following quote, he sounds much like Jung: "There exists a phenomenon...which has puzzled man since the dawn of mythology; the seemingly accidental meeting of two unrelated causal chains in a coincident event which appears both highly improbable and highly significant." Koestler also affirmed the work of another scientist, Australian biologist Paul Kammerer, who did a statistical analysis of hundreds of coincidences and concluded, "There is a basic interconnectedness between things within the deeper patterns of universal laws."

੭ଡ଼ ੭ଡ଼ ੭ଡ଼ ੭ଡ଼

Interestingly, most of the people whose stories are in this book would not use that language. They would say, God is real, God is with us and often gives us a hand in a way that we call coincidence—but could call "miraculous."

I would like to mention one more reflection on coincidence, from a column written by Bill Reel, a columnist for *New York Newsday* (Nov. 27, 1994). Bill had interviewed Fulton Oursler, Jr., editor of *Guideposts,* a spiritual magazine founded by the late Norman Vincent Peale, and the entire column became a story of coincidences that had linked the lives of his family members.

Most Catholics of a generation past remember his father, Fulton Oursler, as being the author of *The Greatest Story Ever Told* and a good Catholic man. But Fulton the son tells how there was no God in their home when he was young and that his father wanted to write a book debunking Christianity. His mother, Grace, was executive editor of *Guideposts* after Peale founded the magazine in 1945.

Young Fulton was sent to a boarding school and hated it. He apparently started sampling some Protestant churches, but wore out his welcome. One night he tried a Catholic parish, met Peggy Jo Reilly, who told him the story of Christ. "Faith seized me that night and has never let go," he told Bill.

The young man began to take instruction, and his favorite place was the grotto in the lower church devoted to St. Bernadette at St. Francis of Assisi church on West Thirty-First Street. It turned out that father and son were in a cab one day and the son noticed it was going in the direction of St. Francis church. He didn't know what to say when they left the cab and went to the grotto. He thought his father had discovered his secret trips there. But to his amazement, his father gave him the shocking news that he himself had become a convert at that grotto.

It was then that his son told him about his own trips here "and the unbelievable coincidence that the grotto where he had found faith was the same one I had so often visited in secret." Tears came to his father's eyes. "He hugged me and said, 'Oh what wonderful tricks the Great Magician plays on us!'"

That wasn't the only coincidence. Fulton Jr. had become an editor at *Reader's Digest*, and stayed there from 1955 to 1987, leaving then to become a freelance writer. But one day in 1991 he got a call from a headhunter asking if he would like to be editor-in-chief of *Guideposts*. The headhunter asked him if he ever heard of the magazine. Indeed, he had. His mother had been the first editor! As he contemplated the offer, he received a letter "out of the blue, from a woman who had been the subject of a piece my mother had written many years before. The woman enclosed a letter my mother had sent a few weeks before her death. It was the first time I had seen my mother's signature in more than thirty-five years." Fulton accepted the job.

Bill Reel ended his column with a quote from Fulton, which aptly summarizes how so many people I've talked to feel about coincidences: "God has a plan for everyone, and it's become an article of faith for me to believe that sometimes we can catch glimpses of the Spirit at work on the grand design through the anonymous miracles of coincidences."

My own reflection after considering all that I have read and all that has been told to me about coincidence in the past years is that we are indeed cared for and loved by a Higher Power, who makes this concern known to us in ways that very often transcend what we think of as "normal." I believe that God is transmitting this message and, to receive it, all we have to do is tune in. When we do, God may be inviting us to a grand surprise party that—left to our earthly resources— we could never have imagined.

∞ ∞ ∞ ∞

Resources

John Leinenweber, *Be Friends of God, Spiritual Readings from Gregory the Great,* Cowley Publications, 1990.

William Styron, *Darkness Visible, A Memoir of Madness,* Random House, 1990.

Patricia Neal, *As I Am, An Autobiography,* Simon & Schuster, 1988.

Konstantine Mochulsky, *Dostoevsky, His Life and Work,* Princeton University Press, 1967.

Eleanor Roosevelt, *This Is My Story,* Harper & Brothers, 1937.

Henry Thomas and Dana Lee Thomas, *50 Great Americans, Their Inspiring Lives and Achievements,* Doubleday, 1948.

Henry Thomas and Dana Lee Thomas, *Living Biographies of Great Scientists,* Garden City Publishing Co., 1941.

Henry Thomas and Dana Lee Thomas, *Living Biographies of Famous Men,* Garden City Publishing Co., 1944.

Rene Vallery-Radot, *The Life of Pasteur,* Doubleday, 1923.

C. Bernard Ruffin, *The Life of Brother André, The Miracle Worker of St. Joseph,* Our Sunday Visitor Publishing Division, 1988.

Jay E. Greene, *Four Biographies [The First Woman Doctor],* Globe Book Co., 1956.

John Carey, Editor, *Eyewitness To History,* Avon Books, 1987.

Peter-Thomas Rohrbach, *The Search for St. Thérèse,* Doubleday, 1961.

Joan Carroll Cruz, *Mysteries, Marvels, Miracles in the Lives of the Saints,* Tan Books and Publishers, 1997.

Viola Meynell, *Francis Thompson and Wilfrid Meynell,* E.P. Dutton, 1953.

Gary Webster, *Wonders of Science, Mysteries That Point to God,* Sheed & Ward, 1956.

Paul Pearsall, *Making Miracles,* Prentice Hall Press, 1991.

V. Gilbert Beers, *Turn Your Hurts Into Healing*, Fleming H. Revell, 1988.

David Matzner, with David Margolis, *The Muselmann, The Diary of a Jewish Slave Laborer*, KATV Publishing House, 1994.

Antoinette Bosco, *The Pummeled Heart, Finding Peace Through Pain*, Twenty-Third Publications, 1994 (later released as *Finding Peace Through Pain, The True Story of a Journey Into Joy*, Ballantine, 1995).

Donal Dorr, *Divine Energy, God Beyond Us, Within Us, Among Us*, Triumph Books, 1996.

Ronald Rolheiser, *The Shattered Lantern, Rediscovering a Felt Presence of God*, Crossroad, 1995.

John Polkinghorne, *Quarks, Chaos & Christianity, Questions to Science and Religion*, Crossroad, 1996.

Jean Shinoda Bolen, M.D., *The Tao of Psychology, Synchronicity and the Self*, Harper Collins, 1979.

C.G. Jung, *Memories, Dreams, Reflections*, Random House, 1961.

Frank Bianco, *Whispers of Silence*, Anchor/Doubleday, 1991.

Murray Sperber, editor, *Arthur Koestler, A Collection of Critical Essays*, Prentice-Hall, Inc., 1969.

James Redfield, *The Celestine Prophecy, An Adventure*, Warner, 1994.

Bridget Mary Meehan, *The Healing Power of Prayer*, Liguori Publications, 1995.

Barbara Hannah, *Jung, His Life and Work, A Biographical Memoir*, G.P. Putnam Sons.

Carl G. Jung, and M.L. von Franz, Joseph Henderson, Jolande Jacobi and Aniela Jaffe, *Man and His Symbols*, Doubleday.

Sigmund Spaeth, *Stories Behind the World's Great Music*, McGraw-Hill Book Co., 1937.

Bernadette "Bunnie" Anderson, *My Father's Will, Out of Grief Into Faith*, published by the author, 1994.

Catherine Beebe, *Saint John Bosco*, Farrar, Straus & Cudahy, 1955.

Bill Reel, "The Reel Story, Anonymous Miracles of Coincidence," *Newsday*, Nov. 27, 1994.

Invitation to Readers:

We invite you to share your own stories of coincidences with us to be included in a possible sequel to this book. Thank you in advance for your response.

Please write your story and send it to:

Antoinette Bosco
Twenty-Third Publications
P.O. Box 180
Mystic, CT 06355

Of Related Interest. . .

The Pummeled Heart
Finding Peace Through Pain
Antoinette Bosco
In this intensely personal sharing of life experiences, Antoinette Bosco takes an honest look at pain. She believes that pain is a wake-up call from God, shaking us out of spiritual complacency and ego-centric lives, and that painful experiences can be catalysts for great personal and spiritual growth.

ISBN: 0-89622-584-4, 140 pp, $7.95

Everyday Epiphanies
Seeing the Sacred in Everything
Melannie Svoboda, SND
Offers 175 short stories with topics ranging from the ordinary to the uncommon occasions that we all look forward to and relish when they occur. A comprehensive index cross references topics and themes to stories. Scripture passages scattered throughout offer insights into the ways that Jesus used the occurrences of everyday living to reveal both God and grace.

ISBN: 0-89622-730-8, 200 pp, $9.95

A World of Stories for Preachers and Teachers
and all who love stories that move and challenge
Rev. William J. Bausch
These newest tales (350!) from Fr. Bausch are not just a plateful of "literary twinkies" but an immense and varied menu with rich meals, wholesome lunches, snacks, and even "Playful Fare." They range in length from several pages to several on one page. *A World of Stories for Preachers and Teachers* should be in the hands of every preacher, storyteller, teacher, and reader—indeed, every person seeking to impart or gain wisdom.

ISBN: 0-89622-919-X, 544 pp, $29.95

Available at religious bookstores or from:

XXIII TWENTY-THIRD PUBLICATIONS

1-800-321-0411

E-Mail:ttpubs@aol.com